AP* U.S. HISTORY
FLASH REVIEW

NEW YORK

Copyright © 2013 LearningExpress, LLC.
All rights reserved under International and Pan
American Copyright Conventions. Published in the
United States by LearningExpress, LLC, New York.

Library of Congress Cataloging-in-Publication Data

AP U.S. history flash review.
     p.   cm.
  ISBN 978-1-57685-919-3
  1. United States—History—Examinations—Study
guides.   2. United States—History—Examinations,
questions, etc.   3. Advanced placement programs
(Education)—Study guides.   4. College entrance
achievement tests—Study guides.   I. LearningExpress
(Organization)   II. Title: U.S. history flash review.
  E178.25.A68   2013
  973.076—dc23

                                        2012032762

Printed in the United States of America

9 8 7 6 5 4 3 2 1

First Edition

ISBN-13: 978-1-57685-919-3

For more information or to place an order, contact
LearningExpress at:
     2 Rector Street
     26th Floor
     New York, NY 10006

Or visit us at:
     www.learningexpressllc.com

CONTENTS

INTRODUCTION

AP U.S. History Flash Review includes 600 names, places, events, and definitions for the AP U.S. History exam. While the subject of the exam is the past, succeeding at the test is great for your future! A good score can improve your chances of being accepted by your top-choice universities. An excellent score may allow you to skip required history courses in college. Studying the key terms in this book is an essential step toward mastering the exam and enjoying all the advantages of your success.

About the AP U.S. History Exam

The AP U.S. History exam is slightly more than three hours long. You will be given 55 minutes to complete the first section, which consists of 80 multiple-choice questions, and 130 minutes to finish the free-response (essay) section. Each section is worth half of your total score for the exam.

The multiple-choice section isn't simply about being able to remember facts. These questions will require you to apply knowledge and analyze information. It is important to know, for example, that Woodrow Wilson was president during World War I. Still, you must also have a general sense of his beliefs about American involvement in the war, some of the policies he instituted to lead America during the crisis, and how he believed the peace treaty should be negotiated.

Each multiple-choice question has five answer choices. There are four types of multiple-choice questions:

- The first type of question will ask you to determine the **cause** of a historical event. Some of these questions will name an event with several causes and then ask you to choose the answer that did *not* cause the event to occur.
- The second type of question will ask you to interpret a **map**. Such questions might show two maps of the same area but from different time periods. Then you might have to determine, for example, what happened to cause any changes you observe between the maps.
- A third type of question will ask you to analyze a photo or an illustration. The AP U.S. History exam often features questions with **political cartoons**. You might be asked to choose the answer that is the best interpretation of the cartoon.
- A fourth question type will display a **chart or graph**. You will be presented with data and be asked to draw a conclusion. For example, if a question offers a graph that shows a region's population increasing sharply over several years, you might be asked to choose the correct reason for the population spike.

The second section of the exam is the free-response, also known as the essay section. You will have a little bit more than two hours to answer three essays. The first essay section is called the Document-Based Question (DBQ). The DBQ will offer an essay prompt and then ask you to consider several primary-source documents in writing an essay response. For example, the DBQ might suggest that the United States had economic reasons for fighting the Spanish-American War. Then you might have to read newspaper editorials from the time, presidential addresses, letters from political leaders, or testimony from the floor of Congress in order to argue whether this statement is correct. For the DBQ, remember to cite evidence from as many of the documents as you can.

The next two essay sections will each ask you to answer one of two standard free-response questions.

For both the DBQ and the two standard essays, remember:

1. Develop a thesis. Have an argument and defend it with evidence. The argument should not be your personal opinion but an informed thesis based on facts that you gather from your historical knowledge.
2. Analyze and interpret—do not summarize. The goal of the essay is to test your ability to recognize concepts and themes in American history, not just your ability to identify facts and summarize events.

3. Address all aspects of the question. The essay prompt, for example, may ask you to consider the economic, social, and political implications of the Monroe Doctrine. Do not write an essay only about the doctrine's effects on the American economy.

The AP U.S. History exam is administered by The College Board, and you can find more information about the test at their website: http://www.college board.com/student/testing/ap/sub_ushist.html.

About This Book

The 600 names, events, terms, and concepts chosen for this book reflect the essential information you'll need to know for your exam. Like the exam, they cover the period from the first European settlements in North America through the present day. Don't worry about events in today's news—the exam focuses primarily on events in the nineteenth and twentieth centuries (1800–2000). About 20% of the exam will cover events before 1790.

You will notice that this book is divided into three sections. The first covers events before 1789, the second focuses on 1790 through 1913, and the third section covers the rest of the twentieth century. Studying terms in roughly chronological order will help you get a sense of your strengths and also what eras you need to study more.

Each page in this book includes three terms that you'll need to know for the AP U.S. History exam.

On the reverse side of each page is that term's description. If the term is the name of a person, location, law, or government agency, then the description will include important biographical information or the term's historical significance. For events, you'll find descriptions that include causes and consequences as well as key dates.

The content of this book reflects the relative percentages of the themes covered on the exam:

- Political and government institutions, political behavior, and public policy: 35%
- Cultural events and social change: 40%
- U.S. diplomacy and international relations: 15%
- Economic history and technological developments: 10%

How to Use This Book

There's no substitute for reading your textbook. Still, it's essential to be able to instantly recall basic information about people, events, and ideas from American history. Quizzing yourself with this book won't help you to learn all there is to know about each term, but you'll certainly be less likely to come across a term on the exam that is completely unfamiliar.

Create a study schedule for yourself. Dedicate 30 minutes each day to reviewing this book, or set a goal by choosing a number of terms to learn each day. Challenge yourself: Add more terms to your daily goal if you're remembering all the key details. Whenever you come across an especially tricky concept or a name that still seems unfamiliar, go back to your textbook.

Don't get frustrated! You already have the skills to succeed at studying American history. Look at the word *history*. Notice the word within the word: "story." Think of the brief story of our country as the plot of your favorite book or TV series. New characters appear. Old characters change, and last season's subplots fade away. Yet, because the characters shared experiences, passions, and ideas, the story builds on itself. That's why you can't stop watching: All the episodes or chapters are connected. And if you look away, you might miss something amazing. American history is closer to you than any novel or TV show because history tells your story.

Think of this book as your guide to the characters, settings, and key plot points of the story of our nation. Maybe you skipped a few chapters in your textbook or missed class because of the flu. Now's your chance to catch up! Once you learn as many of the 600 terms in this book as you can remember, the seemingly long, complicated story of the United States will start to make a lot more sense. These simple facts will help to connect one era to another. And you'll know more than facts—you'll be able to interpret events just as the multiple-choice section will ask you to do. And when it's time to pick up your pen to begin the essay, you'll be ready. You also have a story to tell.

1492–1789

CHRISTOPHER COLUMBUS

. . . .

JUAN PONCE DE LEON

. . . .

AZTECS AND INCAS

An Italian explorer sailing for the Spanish crown whose explorations of the Caribbean made Europeans aware of the Americas, prompting further exploration and settlement.

· ·

A Spanish explorer who explored Florida on two trips to the New World (1513 and 1521) seeking gold; he established Florida as a Spanish colony.

· ·

Powerful civilizations in Central and South America conquered by Spanish conquistadors in the early 1500s.

CONQUISTADORS

. . . .

ENCOMIENDA

. . . .

COLUMBIAN EXCHANGE

Spanish mercenaries who invaded Central and South America during the 1500s and conquered the native Inca and Aztec civilizations.

· ·

A Spanish policy dictating that a Spaniard given land in the New World was responsible for the natives, who essentially became that landowner's property.

· ·

Modern term referring to the exchange of plants, animals, and people between the Old and New World as a result of exploration, colonization, and slavery. European explorers brought back new crops and livestock while tragically bringing European diseases to the New World, which decimated Indian populations.

THE IROQUOIS CONFEDERACY

. . . .

MAGNA CARTA

. . . .

ROANOKE

A military alliance of Indian tribes in the American northeast including Mohawks, Oneidas, Cayugas, and Senecas founded in the late 1500s. As the French and British squabbled over land and trading rights, the confederacy sided with whichever side offered more advantages.

• •

A medieval English document that limited the power of the monarchy, it was a notable influence on colonial government and American constitutional principles.

• •

The colony founded in present-day Virginia in 1585 by Sir Walter Raleigh; all its citizens mysteriously vanished.

HENRY HUDSON

. . . .

VIRGINIA COMPANY

. . . .

JOHN SMITH

The British explorer who navigated what is now New York while sailing on behalf of the Dutch in 1609. His goal was to find a passage to East Asia for Dutch merchants, but he instead discovered what became the Dutch colony of New Amsterdam.

• •

The company established in England in 1607 to establish a permanent colony in America. The result was the founding of Jamestown by Captain John Smith.

• •

Chosen by the Virginia Company to lead the Jamestown Colony in America in 1607.

PROTESTANT REFORMATION

· ·

GLORIOUS REVOLUTION

· ·

PILGRIMS

German monk Martin Luther protested the Catholic Church's insistence that only obeying Church sacraments and doing good works leads to salvation. Luther proposed that faith alone could redeem believers. His protests planted the seeds of the Protestant Reformation.

. . . .

The revolution in England that saw Queen Mary and William of Orange replace King James II, whose repression of the Puritans inspired their emigration to the Americas.

. . . .

A group within the Puritan sect who wished to form a new Protestant church (as opposed to reforming the Church of England from within, which nonseparatist Puritans hoped to do).

PURITANS

. . . .

MAYFLOWER COMPACT

. . . .

JOHN WINTHROP

An Anglican sect that sought to reform the Church of England by ridding it of the trappings of Catholicism. The Pilgrims were a sect within this group who wished to form a new Protestant church.

. . . .

Written by the Pilgrims on their journey to the New World, this agreement established a secular body to govern their new colony. The compact became the basis for the separation of church and state in the American constitution.

. . . .

First governor of the Massachusetts Bay colony from 1630–1649, Winthrop opposed democracy in favor of a more authoritarian government run by religious leaders.

**NEW ENGLAND
CONFEDERATION**

. . . .

MERCANTILISM

. . . .

PLANTATION SYSTEM

A military alliance formed in 1643 between the English colonies of Massachusetts, Plymouth, Connecticut, and New Haven in case of Indian attack.

. . . .

The theory that colonies exist only to supply raw materials to the mother country and to be a market for exported goods.

. . . .

A system of agricultural mass production involving large farms (plantations) and crops like cotton that require processing after harvest. The plantation system in the Americas depended on slave labor for its success.

JOHN CALVIN

. . . .

JOHN LOCKE

. . . .

ADAM SMITH

A French-born intellectual who preached a form of Protestantism that espoused the inherent wickedness of human nature. Calvinists believe that only strict leadership keeps people from sin.

. . . .

An English philosopher of the Enlightenment era, his writings on religious tolerance and the social contract between state and citizen gave birth to modern liberalism and influenced the American founders.

. . . .

A Scottish Enlightenment philosopher who promoted laissez-faire economics, free markets, and supply-and-demand in his treatise *Wealth of Nations*.

THOMAS HOBBES

. . . .

ROGER WILLIAMS

. . . .

ACT OF TOLERATION

A British philosopher who believed that people are motivated primarily by self-interest and fear, and thus they need a strong government to control them—especially a king who could claim divine right to power.

• •

A New England minister who preached that conscience stood above church and state laws. He also spoke against colonists living on territory seized unlawfully from Indians. Williams was banished from the Massachusetts Bay Colony and founded Providence, which would eventually become the colony of Rhode Island.

• •

This 1649 document permitted the practice of all Christian religions in Maryland, which made the colony a haven for Catholics in the New World.

ROYAL CHARTER

. . . .

NAVIGATION LAWS

. . . .

SALEM WITCH TRIALS

A British royal act granting permission to establish a colony. Some charters provided for a king's direct rule of the colony, while others appointed a selected leader or corporation to manage the colony.

. . . .

These royal decrees in the 1660s prevented English colonies from trading with any country other than England.

. . . .

Trials in 1692–1693 that resulted in the execution of 18 people accused of witchcraft in Salem, Massachusetts. An example of religious mass hysteria in the colonies.

BACON'S REBELLION

. . . .

TRIANGULAR TRADE

. . . .

INDENTURED SERVANTS

A rebellion led by Nathaniel Bacon in Virginia during 1676 over the abuse of indentured servants. The incident brought to light social divisions in the colony and ultimately increased calls for African slaves.

• •

A trading scheme largely unauthorized by the British crown by which New England colonists exchanged goods with Caribbean colonists for molasses used to make rum; the rum was then exchanged for African slaves.

• •

To encourage immigration to the American colonies, the indentured servitude system guaranteed 50 acres of land to anyone willing to pay for an Englishman's passage from Europe to the colonies. That sponsored Englishman was obliged to serve his sponsor for a period (usually seven years) before gaining the freedom to seek his own land and employment.

QUAKERS

. . . .

ANNE HUTCHINSON

. . . .

ANTINOMIANISM

A Protestant sect whose members believed that clergy was unnecessary for worship, the Quakers were banished from the Massachusetts Bay Colony and found a haven in William Penn's colony, eventually called Pennsylvania.

• •

Accused of heresy by Puritans for preaching antinomianism and claiming she was divinely inspired, Hutchinson was banished from the Massachusetts Bay Colony in 1638.

• •

The idea that faith alone is necessary for salvation, not obedience to religious law.

SLAVE TRADE

. . . .

MIDDLE PASSAGE

. . . .

DEISM

The trade of enslaved Africans by the British, Dutch, French, and Portuguese for labor in European colonies in the New World. Over several centuries, more than 12 million people were transported to the Americas as slaves.

• •

The transatlantic journey of slaves from Africa to the New World; millions died along the way due to horrific slave ship conditions.

• •

A religious philosophy held by several Founding Fathers, it espouses that rational observation (and not organized religion) can determine the existence, nature, and proper worship of God.

THE ENLIGHTENMENT

. . . .

MOLASSES ACT

. . . .

SUGAR ACT

A European philosophical movement in the eighteenth century that emphasized liberal government, ethics, and science, rather than imagination, emotions, or religion. Many Enlightenment thinkers rejected traditional religious beliefs in favor of Deism, which purports that natural laws govern the world instead of God's intervention.

• •

In an effort to fight the Triangular trade, the British taxed all molasses and sugar imported to the colonies from non-British countries and colonies. Largely ignored or avoided through smuggling, the 1733 tax nonetheless outraged colonists.

• •

In 1764, the British issued another tax on sugar products imported to the colonies that they hoped would be easier to enforce than the Molasses Act. Britain's intensified effort to restrain colonial trade pushed the colonies closer to revolution.

FRENCH AND INDIAN WAR

. . . .

PEACE OF PARIS

. . . .

BOSTON MASSACRE

A war fought from 1754 to 1763 between France and England in their American colonies. The British sought to end French presence in the Americas and through their victory gained French Canada. By removing the French threat, American colonists had less need for English protection.

• •

The 1763 treaty that ended the French and Indian War in the Americas and the Seven Years War in Europe—England gained control of Quebec from France.

• •

In 1770, British soldiers slaughtered Bostonians who were throwing rocks at a custom house in protest of recent royal acts to control the colonies.

TOWN MEETINGS

. . . .

PATRICK HENRY

. . . .

STAMP ACT

An example of participatory democracy common in the colonies; citizens and local government would meet yearly to elect officers, determine taxes, and pass laws.

• •

A notable early voice for independence, this Virginian drew up a list of resolutions in 1765 to resist British oppression. Henry famously said, "Give me liberty or give me death."

• •

A 1765 tax requiring colonists to pay for a stamp on every essential document such as a deed or a mortgage—even playing cards. So severe was the colonists' objection that they organized the Stamp Act Congress, which instituted a boycott of British goods. Eventually Parliament repealed the Stamp Act.

QUARTERING ACT

. . . .

DECLARATORY ACT

. . . .

TOWNSHEND ACTS

English act of 1765 requiring colonists to provide shelter to English soldiers stationed in the Americas.

· ·

In repealing the Stamp Act in 1766, Britain declared that Parliament had the same authority in the colonies as in England, which insinuated to American colonists that further acts and restrictions were coming.

· ·

To raise revenue and punish the colonists for resisting earlier taxes, the 1767 Townshend Acts taxed several popular imports to the colonies, including tea. The colonists were outraged, yet Britain maintained its right to tax them without their consent.

COERCIVE ACTS

. . . .

**INTERNAL VERSUS EXTERNAL
TAXATION**

. . . .

GREAT AWAKENING

In response to colonial protests, England passed these acts to close Boston Harbor and revoke the colonial charter of Massachusetts. Also known as the Intolerable Acts, these decrees inspired the colonists to hold the First Continental Congress.

. . . .

Like the Stamp Act of 1765, an internal tax taxed goods made and sold within the colonies. The colonists preferred external taxation, like the 1764 Sugar Act, which meant merchants were responsible for paying taxes applied to imports.

. . . .

A religious revival in the colonies during the 1770s that saw a wave of preachers delivering passionate sermons very different than the typically unemotional Calvinist worship. The Great Awakening led to the births of the Baptist and Methodists sects.

AP* U.S. HISTORY FLASH REVIEW

JONATHAN EDWARDS

. . . .

TEA ACT

. . . .

SONS OF LIBERTY

A Puritan minister of the First Great Awakening, Edwards led revivals and preached immediate repentance.

. . . .

The 1773 British decree that required the colonies to only buy tea from the East India company, a British monopoly.

. . . .

A group of American patriots including Samuel Adams who organized protests of Parliamentary acts. Their most famous scheme is the Boston Tea Party.

BOSTON TEA PARTY

. . . .

THOMAS PAINE

. . . .

MARQUIS DE LAFAYETTE

When England passed the 1773 Tea Act, protesters in Boston dressed as Indians and stormed a British ship and dumped the tea overboard.

· ·

Author of *Common Sense*, a pamphlet urging the colonies to seek independence. Paine wrote against the abuses of the British government and was instrumental in turning public opinion in favor of the Revolution.

· ·

A French general who aided the colonies during the American Revolution by training and advising the colonial militia.

JOHN DICKINSON

. . . .

GASPEE AFFAIR

. . . .

COMMITTEES OF
CORRESPONDENCE

One of the celebrated writers of American independence, this Pennsylvania lawyer crafted a declaration of colonial rights and grievances in protest of the Townshend Acts. Nonetheless, he refused to sign the Declaration of Independence, believing that the colonies should first complete the Articles of Confederation.

. . . .

When the British customs ship *Gaspee* ran aground in 1772, colonists boarded the ship and destroyed it. Britain demanded that the perpetrators be tried not in a colonial court but in England. This shocking demand inspired the colonists to form Committees of Correspondence.

. . . .

Secret governments organized by American colonies to supersede colonial legislatures and British officials. These committees spread news of colonial resistance and helped communities organize against British loyalists and merchants who complied with oppressive taxation.

FIRST CONTINENTAL CONGRESS

. . . .

SECOND CONTINENTAL CONGRESS

. . . .

LEXINGTON AND CONCORD

The 1774 convention in Philadelphia where 12 of the 13 colonies met to draft a Declaration of Rights and Grievances to King George III. The colonies at this point still acknowledged the right of the British Parliament to regulate trade in the Americas.

. . . .

The 1775 convention where colonial representatives prepared for the inevitable war with England; the convention elected Virginian George Washington to lead the Continental Army.

. . . .

First battles of the American Revolution. American colonists surprised British soldiers seeking to arrest colonial leaders and capture a weapons cache.

PAUL REVERE

. . . .

VIRTUAL REPRESENTATION

. . . .

OLIVE BRANCH PETITION

Famous for riding to warn colonial militiamen about the advance of British soldiers toward Lexington and Concord.

. . . .

As opposed to actual representation in government by elected officials, virtual representation features unelected representatives such as the colonial agents sent to Parliament.

. . . .

The last ditch attempt by the Continental Congress to avoid war with England in 1775. The petition affirmed the loyalty of the colonies to the king and requested that he address their complaints. The petition was refused.

AP* U.S. HISTORY FLASH REVIEW

DECLARATION OF INDEPENDENCE

. . . .

BENEDICT ARNOLD

. . . .

HESSIANS

On July 4, 1776, the Second Continental Congress signed the document that declared the United States an independent nation. Written primarily by Thomas Jefferson, it famously claims: "We hold these truths to be self-evident, that all men are created equal, that they are endowed by their Creator with certain unalienable Rights, that among these are Life, Liberty and the pursuit of Happiness."

. . . .

A general in the Continental army who was caught plotting to surrender to the British in 1778 in exchange for a position in the British military.

. . . .

German soldiers hired by the British during the American Revolution. Some loyalists turned against Britain because of the use of foreign mercenaries against English citizens.

BATTLE OF TRENTON

. . . .

BATTLE OF SARATOGA

. . . .

FRENCH ALLIANCE

After several defeats in New York, the colonial army surprised a Hessian brigade in Trenton, New Jersey. General George Washington crossed the Delaware River with his army on Christmas night in 1776 to achieve the surprise attack, a much-needed victory for colonial forces.

• •

This October 1777 victory for the colonial army in upstate New York led to the surrender of the army of British General John Burgoyne. News of the British defeat compelled France to form a military alliance with the colonists.

• •

France declared itself an American ally when the Battle of Saratoga offered hope of defeating Britain, their longtime enemy in many European wars.

BATTLE OF YORKTOWN

. . . .

ARTICLES OF CONFEDERATION

. . . .

NORTHWEST ORDINANCE

The decisive battle of the American Revolution. Colonial forces and the French navy surrounded British commander Lord Cornwallis at Yorktown, Virginia in 1781. When Cornwallis surrendered, the war was all but won for the colonial army.

． ．

This founding document (before the Constitution) delegated powers (taxation, trade, and military) to individual states, but left the federal government to handle foreign policy and currency. This left the federal government weak and ineffectual, which would later be resolved in a stronger federal Constitution.

． ．

Included in the Articles of Confederation in 1787, this clause created a framework government for the Northwest territory and outlawed slavery in those future states.

ALEXANDER HAMILTON

. . . .

SHAY'S REBELLION

. . . .

FRENCH REVOLUTION

Hamilton served as the first secretary of the treasury. He established the national bank and an economic plan including a tariff, the assumption of state debts, and an excise tax on whiskey (among other goods). He believed industry and manufacturing would strengthen the new nation, as opposed to Jefferson's agrarian vision.

. . . .

A 1786 rebellion in Massachusetts protesting high taxes, debtors' prisons, and the lack of valuable currency. The uprising was quickly quelled, yet it underscored that the lack of a federal constitution prevented the states from protecting the rights of citizens.

. . . .

Inspired in part by the American Revolution, the French overthrew the monarchy of Louis XVII in 1789. What followed was a bloody purge of the nation's aristocracy and several failed democratic governments before Napoleon seized power in 1799.

INDUSTRIAL REVOLUTION

. . . .

SEPARATION OF POWERS

. . . .

JUDICIAL BRANCH

Refers to the mechanization of labor and the rise of the factory system. What began in England during the 1750s with advanced textile machines came to American shores soon thereafter, primarily in the Northeast, where there existed many seaports for receiving raw materials and shipping manufactured goods, as well as rivers to power factories.

• •

The system of checks and balances by which the Constitution divides the government into separate and independent branches. Each has distinct powers and responsibilities so that none has more influence than the others. The three branches are the judicial, executive, and legislative branches.

• •

The judiciary, specifically the Supreme Court, is the final authority on interpreting the Constitution, as well as the constitutionality of state laws. Supreme Court justices are appointed by the President and confirmed by the Senate.

LEGISLATIVE BRANCH

. . . .

EXECUTIVE BRANCH

. . . .

ELECTORAL COLLEGE

The bicameral (two-chambered) American legislature is the Congress, consisting of the House of Representatives and the Senate. Each state elects two senators and also House representatives according to districts based on population. All congressmen and congresswomen are elected by popular vote.

· ·

The president of the United States is the nation's chief executive. The president is elected every four years by the electoral college, a delegate system based on population.

· ·

For fear that an uneducated mob would elect an unfit American president in a direct election, the electoral college was created as a body of delegates who cast votes on behalf of citizens.

FEDERALISTS

. . . .

ANTI-FEDERALISTS

. . . .

MOBOCRACY

Those during the debate over the American Constitution who favored a strong federal government; Federalists often had strong ties to the Northeast and international trade.

. . . .

Those during the debate over the American Constitution who favored states' rights; Anti-Federalists were in general from the agrarian South or western homesteads.

. . . .

During the Constitutional Convention, delegates feared that the uneducated would elect an unsuitable president in a direct election. The Electoral College was born from this fear of rule by the mob.

**LOOSE INTERPRETATION OF
THE CONSTITUTION**

. . . .

**STRICT INTERPRETATION OF
THE CONSTITUTION**

. . . .

THREE-FIFTHS COMPROMISE

Loose interpretation refers to the theory that the government may do what the Constitution does not specifically forbid. President Jefferson justified the Louisiana Purchase by this logic, as the Constitution doesn't permit or prevent the president to purchase territory.

. . . .

Strict interpretation contends that the government may only do what the Constitution specifically allows.

. . . .

Delegates to the Constitutional Convention agreed to allow the Southern slave trade to continue for at least 20 years after ratification and that slaves would count as three-fifths of one person in determining a state's population.

THE FEDERALIST PAPERS

. . . .

FIRST AMENDMENT

. . . .

SECOND AMENDMENT

A series of essays published by John Jay, Alexander Hamilton, and James Madison that urged ratification of the federal Constitution.

• •

Prohibits the establishment of a state religion and guarantees freedom of speech, freedom to assemble, and freedom of the press.

• •

Established the right of the American people to keep and bear arms.

1790–1913

GEORGE WASHINGTON

. . . .

**WASHINGTON'S FAREWELL
ADDRESS**

. . . .

JOHN ADAMS

Military leader of the American Revolution and the first American president (1789–1797). Washington led the foundation of a stable American government by presiding over the drafting of the Constitution. He also kept the young nation out of a war with England by avoiding foreign alliances.

. . . .

Printed in newspapers in 1796; the first outgoing president warned America to avoid foreign alliances (perhaps referring to Jefferson's desire to ally with France) and to refrain from forming political parties.

. . . .

Second president of the United States (1797–1801); coauthor of the Declaration of Independence; negotiated peace with England after the American Revolution; a Federalist who faced fierce opposition from political opponents during his presidency; kept America at peace despite foreign threats.

QUASI-WAR

. . . .

DEMOCRATIC-REPUBLICANS

. . . .

NATURAL RIGHTS
VERSUS LEGAL RIGHTS

PART II

An undeclared 1798–1800 naval war between the United States and France when the Adams administration refused to repay war debts to the new French republic and instead sought trade agreements with England.

. . . .

Political party founded in 1791 by Jefferson and James Madison to oppose the Federalists and Alexander Hamilton's economic policies. The Democratic-Republicans favored states' rights and grew powerful in the South among yeoman farmers and plantation owners.

. . . .

The founders of the United States drew an important distinction between natural rights, inalienable rights granted to all men, and legal rights, laws passed by governments or monarchs that could change.

THOMAS JEFFERSON

. . . .

FUGITIVE SLAVE LAW

. . . .

WHISKEY REBELLION

PART II

Third president (1801–1809); author of the Declaration of Independence; doubled the size of the nation with Louisiana Purchase; pursued aggressive economic policies against England; a Virginia plantation owner with hundreds of slaves who privately struggled with the moral and political implications of slavery.

. . . .

A 1793 law providing for the return of escaped slaves to their owners, the law was strengthened in 1850 to account for the abolitionist movement and the success of the Underground Railroad.

. . . .

A 1794 farmers' rebellion in Pennsylvania against an excise tax on whiskey. When rioters killed federal officers attempting to arrest them, the colonial army intervened. The rebellion demonstrated that the Constitution allowed for a swifter and more authoritative military response than Shay's Rebellion.

JAY TREATY

. . . .

XYZ AFFAIR

. . . .

BANK OF THE UNITED STATES

Treaty ratified in 1793 that avoided conflict between England and the United States. Removed British troops from the Americas and established trading rights for the United States with England and her colonies.

· ·

When Franco-American relations soured in 1800, President Adams sent envoys to France who were secretly told they could only meet with the French foreign minister if they paid a bribe. Adams was outraged and publicized the bribe request.

· ·

Alexander Hamilton created the first national bank in 1791, and its charter was renewed in 1816. Believing that a national bank favored wealthy interests, President Jackson vetoed the act to renew the bank's charter in 1836, which would compel the government to store money in state banks.

BURR CONSPIRACY

. . . .

MIDNIGHT JUDGES

. . . .

ALIEN AND SEDITION ACTS

After killing Alexander Hamilton in a duel, former vice president Aaron Burr joined a mercenary gang in the Louisiana territory. He was captured and accused of seeking Mexican aid for a secession movement in the territories. The Supreme Court acquitted Burr of accusations of treason.

. . . .

On his last night in office in 1801, President John Adams stayed up until midnight appointing Federalist judges to federal court posts so that his party might maintain influence in the new Democratic-Republican government led by Thomas Jefferson.

. . . .

Passed by Congress and President Adams in 1798, these laws lengthened the waiting period for citizenship, empowered the government to arrest dangerous foreigners, and made it illegal to publish defamatory statements about the government. A response to the XYZ Affair, these laws were largely ineffectual and unenforced.

SECOND GREAT AWAKENING

. . . .

LOUISIANA PURCHASE

. . . .

LEWIS AND CLARK

PART II

Starting around 1801, this religious revival led by Baptist and Methodist sects preached tolerance of new Protestant faiths and drew more participation from women, blacks, and Indians.

· ·

President Jefferson purchased the land from the Mississippi River to the Rocky Mountains from French emperor Napoleon in 1803, which doubled the size of the United States, provided valuable shipping lanes, and gave the growing nation room to expand.

· ·

Two explorers who embarked on the first major exploration of the American west in 1804–1806. Traveling from the Missouri River to the Pacific, they mapped the region and collected valuable information about resources they discovered in the new Louisiana Purchase.

MARBURY v. MADISON

. . . .

JOHN MARSHALL

. . . .

ELASTIC CLAUSE

An 1803 Supreme Court case that helped to define the constitutional boundary between the judicial and executive branches of government. The case increased the power of the courts by establishing that the judiciary interprets what the Constitution allows, which is called judicial review.

• •

Chief Justice of the United States from 1801 to 1835, Marshall was hugely influential in establishing the Supreme Court as a branch of government equal to the legislature and the executive branch. Marshall's opinions are the foundation for much American constitutional law and established judicial review, which allows the Court to decide the constitutionality of laws.

• •

The Constitution states that Congress has the ability "to make all laws which shall be necessary and proper for carrying into execution the foregoing powers." This so-called "elastic clause" gives unspecified or implied powers to Congress, which has been the source of much debate over the extent of the legislature's authority.

TRIPOLITAN WAR

. . . .

ROBERT FULTON

. . . .

FIRST PARTY SYSTEM

PART II

A small naval war launched against Tripoli and Algeria in 1801 to stop pirate attacks on American ships. Neither the United States nor its opponents were truly victorious, and the United States continued to pay the tribute demanded by the North African states to protect American ships.

. . . .

Fulton constructed the first steamboat in the United States in 1807 and also designed the first practical submarine.

. . . .

Describes the first American political party structure from 1792 to 1824, when the Federalists and Democratic-Republicans vied for power. Federalists controlled government until 1800, but Jefferson's Democratic-Republicans held sway after his election.

JAMES MADISON

. . . .

TECUMSEH

. . . .

JAMES MONROE

Fourth president (1809–1817); a *Federalist Papers* writer; principal author of the Bill of Rights and Constitution; led the United States into the War of 1812.

· ·

A Shawnee chief who united the Northwestern Indian tribes against invading settlers, Tecumseh was defeated by an American army led by William Henry Harrison at the Battle of Tippecanoe in 1811.

· ·

Fifth president (1817–1825); remembered for the Monroe Doctrine to keep Europe from intervening in American affairs; presided over a relatively peaceful period but for the Panic of 1819.

JOHN QUINCY ADAMS

· ·

NAPOLEONIC WARS

· ·

THE WAR OF 1812

PART II

The sixth president (1825–1829); son of John Adams; expert diplomat who negotiated peace after the War of 1812 and oversaw annexation of Florida; author of Monroe Doctrine; the only president to serve in Congress after leaving office; became a fierce political opponent of slavery.

• •

The wars declared by several European coalitions against Napoleon's French empire between 1803 and 1815. The War of 1812 is seen as an extension of these wars in the Americas.

• •

War between the United States and England over British trade restrictions for American goods, as well as British seizure of American ships. The defeated British signed the Treaty of Ghent in 1814, which allowed for free American trade in Europe.

IMPRESSMENT

. . . .

HARTFORD CONVENTION

. . . .

ESSEX JUNTO

One of the causes of the War of 1812; British naval ships would capture American merchant marine vessels searching for deserters. The British would force anyone who could not prove he was an American citizen into service of the British navy.

• •

New England merchants who opposed trade restriction and the War of 1812 met in Hartford in 1814 to advocate for the right of states to nullify federal laws. The convention also discussed seceding from the United States if these demands were not met, which turned public sentiment against the Federalist Party.

• •

Extreme Federalist critics of the War of 1812 who advocated the secession of New England from the United States.

NATIONALISM

. . . .

ERA OF GOOD FEELINGS

. . . .

TARIFF

PART II

A belief that loyalty to the nation is of utmost political importance. After the American victory in the War of 1812, more people referred to themselves as Americans rather than citizens of their state or region.

. . . .

After the War of 1812, a lull in political conflict as well as a burst of nationalism and economic growth, which seemed markedly different than earlier years of war and partisan strife.

. . . .

A federal government-imposed tax on imported goods to protect domestic manufacturers. Also referred to as "customs."

TARIFF OF 1816

. . . .

SEMINOLE INDIANS

. . . .

THE PANIC OF 1819

By raising the price of higher-quality yet often cheaper British imported goods, this protective tariff boosted American manufacturing.

· ·

Indian tribe in Florida encouraged by the Spanish to raid American settlements in 1817. President John Quincy Adams sent Andrew Jackson to lead a military operation against the Seminoles, and his success helped convince the Spanish to cede the territory to the United States.

· ·

Blame for this economic depression fell on the national bank, though economists now see the panic as caused by overproduction following the War of 1812.

FRANCIS CABOT LOWELL

. . . .

JOHN JACOB ASTOR

. . . .

TALLMADGE AMENDMENT

PART II

Introduced the mechanized textile industry to the United States at his Massachusetts factories, a key early step in the American Industrial Revolution.

. . . .

Fur-trading magnate who helped finance the War of 1812, Astor was the nation's first multimillionaire.

. . . .

Preceding the 1820 compromise on slavery in the new state of Missouri, the Tallmadge Amendment would have admitted Missouri with its existing slave population but would free all slave children at age 25. The proposal was rejected.

MISSOURI COMPROMISE

. . . .

MONROE DOCTRINE

. . . .

ERIE CANAL

PART
II

A compromise between pro- and anti-slavery factions, Missouri was admitted as a slave state in 1820 while Maine would enter the union as a free state (no slavery). The compromise also declared that slavery would be illegal in all territory north of the 36°30" latitude and legal to the south.

. . . .

President James Monroe's address to Congress in 1823 that warned European powers to stay out of the Americas and demanded nonintervention in current European colonies in Latin America.

. . . .

Opened in 1825, the Erie Canal created a key shipping lane between New York and the Great Lakes and helped further western expansion.

HENRY CLAY

· ·

JOHN C. CALHOUN

· ·

ANDREW JACKSON

Kentucky Senator who proposed the Missouri Compromise, which admitted Missouri as a slave state and Maine as a free state, so long as slavery would be illegal thereafter in all states north of an appointed line of latitude.

. . . .

Jackson's vice president and South Carolina senator who argued that the North should not interfere with slavery where it already existed. Calhoun was a tireless advocate of states' rights.

. . . .

Seventh president (1829–1837), Jackson had humble beginnings. Orphaned at 14 and never formerly educated, he nonetheless became a formidable general and politician. Jacksonian democracy refers to the increased political involvement of the common man in govern-ment, captured in the election of 1828, which swept Jackson into office with the largest ever popular vote at the time.

JACKSONIAN DEMOCRACY

. . . .

TARIFF OF ABOMINATIONS

. . . .

NULLIFICATION

Refers to the sociopolitical changes inspired by the election of Andrew Jackson, who opposed monopolies and the privileged class of society and urged increased popular participation in government and greater opportunity for the common man.

. . . .

Southern term for the tariff of 1828, a tax on imported manufactured goods. Southerners felt the tax passed due to the influence of New England mercantile interests, and the debate led to calls for nullification.

. . . .

In response to the tariff of 1828, Vice President Calhoun anonymously published an essay proposing that states had the right to nullify an unconstitutional act of Congress. This policy, Calhoun thought, would quiet calls for secession from South Carolina over the hated tariff.

AP* U.S. HISTORY FLASH REVIEW

PART II

DANIEL WEBSTER

. . . .

GIBBONS v. OGDEN

. . . .

ELI WHITNEY

A powerful orator, this Massachusetts senator was one of the most influential men in Congress before the Civil War. A father of American conservatism, Webster argued vociferously against the rise of Jacksonian democracy and strove to protect the interests of New England shipping and merchants as well as banking and industrialization.

• •

Landmark Supreme Court ruling in 1824 that affirmed federal authority to regulate interstate commerce. Daniel Webster argued for the winning cause.

• •

Inventor of the cotton gin in 1793, a device that mechanized the painstaking process of removing seeds from cotton. It allowed for a boom in cotton production and thus bolstered the need for African slaves.

CYRUS MCCORMICK

. . . .

CLIPPER SHIPS

. . . .

ANTI-MASONS

PART II

Inventor of the mechanical reaper, which revolutionized American agriculture in 1831.

. . . .

These American ships built during the 1840s were fast and maneuverable and boosted American trade, especially with China.

. . . .

When a prominent Freemason was murdered after he left the secret society, this party formed as an anti-elitist effort to oppose the supposed influence of the Masons in government. As the first major American third party, the Anti-Masons ran presidential candidates in 1832 and 1836 and introduced nominating conventions and the concept of party platforms to American politics.

NICOLAS BIDDLE

. . . .

PET BANK

. . . .

KITCHEN CABINET

The corrupt president of the national bank who issued loans as bribes, which inspired President Jackson to turn against the bank.

. . . .

In vetoing the charter renewal for the Bank of the United States in 1836, Jackson deposited federal funds into state banks (referred to as his "pet banks") because he claimed a national bank catered to wealthy and foreign interests.

. . . .

The dismissive name for the friends and advisors from whom President Jackson sought advice instead of consulting his cabinet.

SPECIE CIRCULAR

. . . .

THE PANIC OF 1837

. . . .

MARTIN VAN BUREN

PART II

This 1836 act stated that all public lands must be purchased with gold or silver currency due to the failure of the national bank and the devaluation of paper currency. The subsequent run on gold and silver spurned the Panic of 1837.

. . . .

When President Jackson declared that payment for federal lands must be in gold or silver instead of currency from the national bank, the bank failed, prices of commodities like cotton plummeted, and businesses went bankrupt.

. . . .

Eighth president (1837–1841), the first born an American citizen; presided over strained relations with England and the Panic of 1837, which tainted his legacy.

AP* U.S. HISTORY FLASH REVIEW

WILLIAM HENRY HARRISON

. . . .

JOHN TYLER

. . . .

MANIFEST DESTINY

Ninth president (1841); a military hero for defeating Tecumseh at the Battle of Tippecanoe, his death in office after a month as president sparked a constitutional crisis about succession.

• •

Tenth president (1841–1845); a Virginian aristocrat who sided with the confederacy later in life, as president he endeavored to annex the Republic of Texas.

• •

The concept that the destiny of the United States was to expand across the continent to the Pacific. Used as justification for the Mexican-American War.

OREGON TRAIL

. . . .

ALEXIS DE TOCQUEVILLE

. . . .

WHIGS

The main route in the Oregon territory, which was swarmed by easterners and midwesterners in the 1840s seeking free land and a fresh start.

. . . .

Author of a two-part book on American democracy, this Frenchmen traveling in the United States observed the advantages of American democracy and offered a revealing look at the developing nation's character.

. . . .

A largely conservative party favored by the upper class, the Whigs emerged from the National Republican Party and Federalists in the 1830s. They won many votes from supporters of the national bank and southern plantation owners for their support of industry and tariffs. Prominent Whigs included Henry Clay and Daniel Webster.

DOROTHEA DIX

. . . .

HORACE MANN

. . . .

AMERICAN TEMPERANCE SOCIETY

A reformer responsible for improving conditions in jails, poorhouses, and insane asylums, Dix began in the 1820s to lobby for states to assume care of the mentally ill.

. . . .

Using Prussian military academies as a model, this New England education reformer started the American public school movement in Massachusetts, where he instituted a school system that became the envy of the nation.

. . . .

A society to promote abstinence from alcohol that spread quickly after its founding in 1826 to promote awareness of the evils of drinking.

PART II

MAINE LAW

. . . .

JOSEPH SMITH

. . . .

BRIGHAM YOUNG

The first major legislative success for the Temperance Movement; Maine outlawed the sale of alcohol except for medical and religious purposes in 1851. The law was unpopular and repealed five years later.

. . . .

Founder of the Latter-day Saints movement and author of the Book of Mormon, Smith developed the faith that became Mormonism and led his followers as they were expelled from settlements in Ohio and Missouri. He was killed during mob violence before he could reach his vision of establishing a theocratic settlement outside of U.S. government control.

. . . .

Leader of the Latter-day Saints movement, Young led the Mormons to what he called their Promised Land in Utah, where he founded Salt Lake City and became the territory's first governor.

INDIAN REMOVAL ACT

. . . .

TRAIL OF TEARS

. . . .

CHEROKEE NATION v. GEORGIA

This 1830 law signed by Andrew Jackson forcibly relocated over 100,000 American Indians from their land to areas designated by the government.

. . . .

When the U.S. Army relocated Georgia's Cherokee Indians to Oklahoma Indian territory, many died under harsh conditions on the forced march. The 1838–1839 incident became a symbol of the abuse of American Indians.

. . . .

In 1831, the Cherokee Nation sued Georgia for depriving them of territorial rights, but the Supreme Court refused to rule, saying "the relationship of the tribes to the United States resembles that of a 'ward to its guardian.'"

TRANSCENDENTALISTS

. . . .

HENRY DAVID THOREAU

. . . .

"ON CIVIL DISOBEDIENCE"

Thinkers and artists who emphasized a spiritual philosophy centered on the connection between mankind and nature, the transcendentalists encouraged self-reliance and discouraged materialism. Henry David Thoreau (author of *Walden*) and Ralph Waldo Emerson captured this movement in writing.

. . . .

Massachusetts writer and notable figure in the transcendentalist movement, Thoreau is remembered for his essay on civil disobedience, which encourages resistance against an unjust government.

. . . .

Henry David Thoreau's 1849 essay that introduced the concept of passive resistance. In protest of the Mexican-American War, Thoreau refused to pay taxes and was sent to jail. He urged readers to fight unjust laws simply by disobeying them.

NATHANIEL HAWTHORNE

....

WALT WHITMAN

....

HORACE GREELEY

Rejecting the transcendentalist views of many fellow writers of his era, Hawthorne is best known as author of *The Scarlet Letter*. This novel seems to criticize the sanctimonious streak in American religion by portraying the cruelty of Puritans against an adulterous woman, who they force to wear a scarlet A.

• •

American poet who democratized poetry by using colloquial language, Whitman's "Leaves of Grass" (1855) was banned for celebrating bodily pleasures, which many found immoral.

• •

In the newspaper he founded, the *New York Tribune*, Greely popularized the notion that poor men on the East Coast could make their fortunes by going west to seek opportunity on the frontier.

ONEIDA COMMUNE

. . . .

SENECA FALLS

. . . .

SUFFRAGE

A socioreligious movement based in New York. The members were polygamous, shared property communally, and collectively raised their children.

• •

Site of the 1848 women's rights convention where Elizabeth Cady Stanton issued a declaration recounting the discrimination of women and urging women's suffrage.

• •

The right to vote. Originally granted only to white male Americans, this constitutional right was extended to black men in 1870 and women in 1920.

ELIZABETH CADY STANTON

. . . .

SUSAN B. ANTHONY

. . . .

CULT OF DOMESTICITY

A prominent early advocate for a women's suffrage movement, she organized the 1848 convention at Seneca Falls for women's rights and edited the first feminist newspaper, *The Revolution.*

. . . .

Social activist and cofounder of the Women's Temperance Movement, she was a tireless advocate for women's rights to be recognized by the U.S. government and owner of *The Revolution.*

. . . .

A cultural credo of the mid-nineteenth century that glorified women as pious, respectful, and virtuous keepers of a domestic sanctuary for husbands and children. This concept restricted women to the home and insisted that women and men live in separate spheres.

FORTY-NINERS

. . . .

JAMES KNOX POLK

. . . .

ZACHARY TAYLOR

Americans from the East who flocked to California in 1849 when gold was discovered.

. . . .

Eleventh president (1845–1849); led the nation into Mexican-American War, gaining what would become the current southwest states, and also settled a dispute with England over Oregon Territory.

. . . .

Twelfth president (1849–1850), military hero of the War of 1812, the Mexican-American War and Indian campaigns; a slave owner who nonetheless accepted new slavery-free states and presided over the Compromise of 1850. Died in office.

REPUBLIC OF TEXAS

. . . .

STEPHEN AUSTIN

. . . .

THE ALAMO

Texas declared itself a sovereign nation in 1836. Economic and territorial strife forced Texas to seek annexation into the United States in 1845.

. . . .

Founder of the first American settlement in Texas in 1822, Austin negotiated Texan independence from Mexico and eventually led the Texas Revolution for the territory's independence.

. . . .

When the Mexican army attacked this Texas fort in 1836 and killed every American resister after a 13-day standoff, "Remember the Alamo!" became a battle cry in the Texas Republic's struggle for independence.

SANTA ANNA

. . . .

SAM HOUSTON

. . . .

MEXICAN WAR

Mexican military and political leader who defeated Texan forces at the Alamo in 1836, he was later defeated and forced to sign a treaty allowing the Republic of Texas to declare itself independent, paving the way for Texas to eventually become an American territory.

. . . .

First commander of the Texas army, Houston served as the territory's president and advocated Texas joining the Union in 1845. He was ousted as governor of Texas in 1861 for refusing to allow Texas to join the Confederacy.

. . . .

When the United States annexed Texas in 1845, Mexico declared war, claiming right to the territory. The victorious United States won not only Texas but also Utah, California, Nevada, Arizona, and New Mexico.

TREATY OF GUADALUPE HIDALGO

. . . .

WILMOT PROVISO

. . . .

OSTEND MANIFESTO

This treaty ended the Mexican War in 1848 and granted the United States the rights to Texas, California, Utah, Nevada, Arizona, and New Mexico for the cost of $18 million. The treaty also drew the border of the United States and Mexico at the Rio Grande.

• •

Congress failed to pass this furiously debated 1846 act that would have outlawed slavery in any territory America won during the Mexican War. It became a symbol of the intensity of the abolition debate.

• •

Diplomatic memo in 1854 urging the annexation of Cuba that inflamed debate over American expansionism and the spread of slavery.

POPULAR SOVEREIGNTY

. . . .

KANSAS-NEBRASKA ACT

. . . .

MILLARD FILLMORE

PART
II

A term meaning that citizens of each state had the right to decide their own laws by voting. Popular sovereignty was important during the debate over slavery, which was often declared legal or illegal for particular states by federal decree.

. . . .

Act that created the territories of Kansas and Nebraska in 1854 but overturned the Missouri Compromise by allowing voters in the new territories to determine via popular sovereignty whether to allow slavery.

. . . .

Thirteenth president (1850–1853); pursued trade with Japan and China; after leaving the White House later ran for president again for the nativist Know-Nothing Party.

FRANKLIN PIERCE

. . . .

GADSDEN PURCHASE

. . . .

GERMAN AND IRISH IMMIGRATION

PART II

Fourteenth president (1853–1857); responsible for unpopular decisions like the Kansas-Nebraska Act and the Ostend Manifesto, which inflamed sectional politics and the divide over slavery.

. . . .

A purchase from Mexico in 1853 of important stagecoach routes in the Southwest, which included large portions of what became New Mexico and Arizona.

. . . .

The first wave of immigrants to the United States during the nineteenth century came from Germany and Ireland. Driven by the Great Famine, Irish immigration peaked after 1845. Germans came in large numbers after 1850, with peak years in the 1880s.

NATIVISTS

. . . .

KNOW-NOTHING PARTY

. . . .

ANTEBELLUM

Those who were disturbed by the influx of foreigners moving to the United States during the nineteenth century and favored restrictions on immigration.

. . . .

A secretive party of anti-foreign and anti-Catholic nativists who nominated the former president Millard Fillmore in 1865. Their slogan: "Americans must rule America!"

. . . .

Literally meaning "before the war," this term refers to the period from the 1790s to the Civil War.

NAT TURNER'S REBELLION

. . . .

SOJOURNER TRUTH

. . . .

THE UNDERGROUND RAILROAD

PART II

The 1831 slave uprising led by Nat Turner, who believed he was divinely chosen to free other slaves. The rebellion killed 60 whites in Virginia. A violent manhunt ensued to kill the perpetrators, and southern states strengthened their demand for stronger fugitive slave laws and other restrictions against blacks.

• •

Born a slave in New York around 1797, Sojourner Truth went on to become one of the most powerful abolitionist voices as well as a voice of the nascent women's rights movement. She is also remembered as one of the first black women to win a court case against a white man.

• •

A secretive network of abolitionists who organized escape routes for runaway slaves to get to free states in the North.

HARRIET TUBMAN

. . . .

FREDRICK DOUGLASS

. . . .

WILLIAM LLOYD GARRISON

PART II

Tubman, herself an escaped slave, helped hundreds of slaves escape bondage as a leader of the Underground Railroad.

• •

Born a slave, Douglass educated himself and escaped slavery in 1838 to become one of the abolitionist movement's best-known orators. He edited the abolitionist newspaper called *The North Star*.

• •

Militant abolitionist and publisher of a radical anti-slavery newspaper in Boston who urged Northern secession from the United States in protest of slavery.

FREE-SOIL PARTY

. . . .

COMPROMISE OF 1850

. . . .

HARRIET BEECHER STOWE

Party founded in 1847 opposing the existence of slavery in any new American state or territory.

. . . .

Compromise that avoided Southern secession temporarily, admitted California as a free state, abolished slavery in the District of Columbia, allowed the New Mexico and Utah territories to decide slavery via popular sovereignty, and toughened fugitive slave laws.

. . . .

Author of the abolitionist novel *Uncle Tom's Cabin* (1852), which some call an inspiration for the Civil War by so effectively capturing the divide over slavery.

BLEEDING KANSAS

. . . .

DRED SCOTT v. SANDFORD

. . . .

JOHN BROWN

PART
II

A four-year skirmish during the 1850s between pro-slavery Kansans and abolitionists in Missouri along the border between these states.

· ·

Scott, a Missouri slave, sued for his freedom in 1857, claiming that he was free by virtue of having lived for a time in the northern portion of the Louisiana Territory made free land by the Missouri Compromise. The U.S. Supreme Court ruled he couldn't sue in federal court because he was not a citizen but property.

· ·

A militant abolitionist who seized the military arsenal at Harper's Ferry, Virginia, in 1859, Brown plotted to end slavery by murdering slave owners and freeing their slaves.

HARPER'S FERRY

. . . .

STEPHEN DOUGLAS

. . . .

CRITTENDEN COMPROMISE

Virginia site of the military arsenal captured in 1859 by militant abolitionist John Brown, who plotted to murder slave owners.

. . . .

Politician famous for his debates on slavery with Abraham Lincoln, Douglas advocated annexation of Mexico and supported the Compromise of 1850.

. . . .

An 1860 proposal to avoid civil war by creating a constitutional amendment guaranteeing slavery's existence in the South and noninterference by Congress in current slave states. The Republicans refused to ratify it.

JAMES BUCHANAN

. . . .

ABRAHAM LINCOLN

. . . .

EMANCIPATION
PROCLAMATION

PART
II

Fifteenth president (1857–1861), he could not settle the deep divides that had been building for decades between the North and South.

. . . .

Sixteenth president (1861–1865); led the nation through the Civil War and ended slavery. An eloquent speaker and author of the Gettysburg Address, a brilliant and open-minded statesman who surrounded himself with opposing viewpoints, and a shrewd commander-in-chief who oversaw a successful campaign to end the Confederacy. First president to be assassinated, in 1865.

. . . .

President Lincoln issued this proclamation in 1862, which freed all slaves in territories that had not seceded from the United States.

JEFFERSON DAVIS

. . . .

ROBERT E. LEE

. . . .

CONFEDERATE STATES OF AMERICA

President of the Confederate States of America, which he led from 1861 to 1865.

. . . .

The leader of the army of the Confederate States of America.

. . . .

Eleven slave states that seceded from the Union in 1861 formed a new nation with Jefferson Davis as acting president. No foreign nation recognized the legitimacy of the Confederacy as an independent state.

COPPERHEADS

. . . .

FORT SUMTER

. . . .

BULL RUN

Lincoln's term for antiwar Northern Democrats, whom he believed to be traitors waiting for an opportunity to strike against him—like a poisonous copperhead snake.

. . . .

Site of the opening battle of the Civil War, this Union-controlled South Carolina fort was besieged by Confederate forces in 1861. The attack forced Congress to declare war on the Confederate States of America.

. . . .

The first major battle of the Civil War began at Bull Run when Confederate soldiers surprised Union soldiers en route to Richmond, Virginia, and forced them to retreat to Washington.

ANTIETAM

. . . .

GETTYSBURG

. . . .

ULYSSES S. GRANT

The aftermath of this Civil War victory for Union forces in 1862 was significant: The Confederate campaign to invade Maryland was ended, Lincoln felt confident enough to issue the Emancipation Proclamation, and Britain and France decided against recognizing the Confederate States of America.

· ·

The turning point of the Civil War, Robert E. Lee's invasion of the North in 1863 was rebuffed at Gettysburg, Pennsylvania, where Lincoln later paid tribute to fallen Union soldiers in his Gettysburg Address.

· ·

Eighteenth president (1869–1877), commander of the Union Army during the Civil War. Despite his initial sympathy for Radical Republicans, Grant could not prevent conservatives from regaining political control of the South.

CLARA BARTON

. . . .

DRAFT RIOTS

. . . .

THIRTEENTH AMENDMENT

The Civil War nurse who later founded the American Red Cross.

. . . .

The United States enforced a compulsory draft for the Union Army, and poor Americans were disproportionately forced to serve, which led to riots around the nation. The largest riots in New York led to over 70 deaths in 1863.

. . . .

Ratified in 1865, this amendment abolished slavery.

WILLIAM TECUMSEH SHERMAN

. . . .

JOHN WILKES BOOTH

. . . .

RECONSTRUCTION

PART II

Union general who drove his army through Georgia and South Carolina, destroying key infrastructure and crops in order to break the Confederacy's morale.

• •

An actor by trade, Booth assassinated Abraham Lincoln in Washington's Ford Theater as the president watched a play. Booth was captured and killed several days later.

• •

The period from 1865 to 1877 during which the federal government administered the rebuilding of civil structures and equal society in the South. The effort is largely considered a failure, as racist institutions replaced slavery and widespread poverty afflicted southerners of all races.

ANDREW JOHNSON

. . . .

FREEDMEN

. . . .

FREEDMAN'S BUREAU

Seventeenth president (1865–1869); presided over Reconstruction; considered too conciliatory toward the former Confederate states and did little to protect the civil rights of former slaves; impeached by the House of Representatives.

. . . .

A term referring to former slaves, especially after the Civil War ended American slavery.

. . . .

This agency provided food and clothing to impoverished former slaves and helped them to adjust to life as freedmen.

FOURTEENTH AMENDMENT

....

CARPETBAGGERS

....

SCALAWAGS

Grants full citizenship to all native-born and naturalized immigrants, as well as former slaves. Ratified in 1868 as part of Reconstruction.

. . . .

A pejorative term for northerners who came to the South during Reconstruction to gain wealth by buying land from desperate southerners and manipulating black voters to obtain government contracts.

. . . .

A pejorative term for southerners who cooperated with the North to purchase land from desperate southerners during Reconstruction.

FIFTEENTH AMENDMENT

. . . .

SHARECROPPERS

. . . .

RADICAL REPUBLICANS

PART II

This 1870 amendment to the Constitution denied states the right to change their own constitutions to limit black suffrage. It guaranteed the right to vote for all Americans regardless of race.

· ·

Hardly better than slavery for blacks after the Civil War, sharecropping was an exploitative system. Plantation owners would grant land to former slaves in exchange for a share of the freedmen's crops.

· ·

A northern political faction whose members believed that moderate Republicans were not harsh enough with former Confederate states. The radicals favored punitive policies against Confederate leaders and full civil rights for former slaves.

THADDEUS STEVENS

. . . .

RECONSTRUCTION ACTS

. . . .

COMPROMISE OF 1877

Leader of the Radical Republicans in Congress who argued for harsh punishments for the South after the Civil War.

. . . .

Despite a veto by President Andrew Johnson, Radical Republicans pushed through these acts which divided the former Confederacy into military districts controlled by a general.

. . . .

Alleged agreement between members of Congress to decide the 1876 election. The deal awarded Republican Rutherford B. Hayes the electoral votes he needed to win the presidency so long as he agreed to remove federal troops from southern states, effectively ending Reconstruction.

RUTHERFORD B. HAYES

. . . .

MARK TWAIN

. . . .

SAMUEL F.B. MORSE

PART II

Nineteenth president (1877–1891); elected controversially as he lost the popular vote but was awarded 20 electoral votes as part of an agreement to remove federal troops occupying former Confederate capitols; quelled the Railroad Strike of 1877 and instituted civil service reform.

. . . .

Author of *The Adventures of Tom Sawyer* and *Adventures of Huckleberry Finn*, Twain's humorous and often satirical tales captured the language and lives of ordinary Americans.

. . . .

Inventor who designed the telegraph system and Morse code, which was adopted worldwide in the mid-1800s to send telegraph messages, the first real-time communications technology.

TRANSATLANTIC TELEGRAPH CABLE

. . . .

COMMODORE PERRY

. . . .

PONY EXPRESS

Finished in 1858, this undersea cable between Canada and Ireland enabled the first near-instant communication between Europe and the Americas.

. . . .

U.S. naval commander who forcefully convinced Japan to open its ports to trade with the United States in 1853.

. . . .

Mail service started in 1860 to deliver letters from Missouri to California, a 2,000-mile trip that the fastest riders could finish in 10 days.

TRANSCONTINENTAL RAILROAD

. . . .

HOMESTEAD ACT

. . . .

PANIC OF 1873

PART II

In May 1869, the Union Pacific and Central Pacific railroads met in Utah, and a railway spanning the entire continent was complete.

. . . .

The 1862 decree meant to encourage western migration by offering free land for settlers in the western territories.

. . . .

Overspeculation in railroads and an international drop in the value of silver led to a huge financial collapse. Banks shut down and the New York Stock Exchange temporarily closed. Unemployment reached 14%.

GREENBACKS

. . . .

GREENBACK PARTY

. . . .

FREDERICK JACKSON TURNER

PART II

Paper currency issued by the Union during the Civil War that was not backed by silver or gold.

. . . .

Antimonopoly, pro-union party active in the 1870s and 1880s, they rejected the shift from paper money back to gold- or silver-based currency because they believed that banks and corporations would have the power to determine the value of goods and labor.

. . . .

This historian's frontier thesis held that civilization would advance so long as there was territory to explore, as new frontiers provide opportunities for homeless or otherwise unsettled men who are the causes of social problems.

INDIAN APPROPRIATIONS ACT

. . . .

CHIEF JOSEPH

. . . .

BATTLE OF LITTLE BIGHORN

PART
II

Federal reorganization of Indian land in 1851 that created the reservation system.

. . . .

Leader of Nez Perce tribe, which battled the U.S. military during attempts to relocate them to an Idaho reservation in 1870.

. . . .

1876 battle in which a coalition of Sioux and Cheyenne Indians led by a chief called Sitting Bull wiped out General George Custer's troops.

DAWES ACT

· ·

WOUNDED KNEE

· ·

WILLIAM SEWARD

PART II

Legislation in 1887 meant to assimilate Indians by encouraging them to purchase tribal land from the government to maintain their autonomy.

. . . .

South Dakota site of the 1890 massacre of several hundred Lakota Sioux Indians.

. . . .

Secretary of State Seward, a passionate expansionist, urged the purchase of Alaska from Russia in 1886. The Alaska acquisition was called "Seward's folly," yet turned out to be a valuable territory supplying timber, gold, and oil.

CIVIL RIGHTS ACT OF 1875

. . . .

JIM CROW LAWS

. . . .

GRANDFATHER CLAUSES

PART II

The Supreme Court decided this act was unconstitutional; its purpose was to outlaw Jim Crow laws and make public discrimination against blacks illegal.

. . . .

State laws that created racial segregation in the South by restricting voting rights for black Americans and segregated public facilities.

. . . .

A scheme to deny voting rights to blacks, these local rules in the South allowed a citizen to vote only if his grandfather had been able to vote. As freed slaves or the sons of freedmen, blacks had no ancestors who could vote and were thus disenfranchised.

W.E.B. DUBOIS

. . . .

THE ATLANTA COMPROMISE

. . . .

LYNCHING

A founder of the National Association for the Advancement of Colored People (NAACP), DuBois was a fiery orator who opposed compromise on race relations and demanded full civil rights for blacks long before the concept seemed reasonable even to many blacks themselves. He opposed the Atlanta Compromise.

• •

An 1895 accord between black leaders and southern political figures that offered a compromise on race relations: Southern blacks would submit to white political rule and end calls for integration, while southern whites would guarantee basic education and legal due process for blacks.

• •

A frighteningly common exercise in mob justice, lynching describes the execution (usually by hanging) of an alleged lawbreaker without due process. Blacks who seemed to disobey or insult whites in the South were often the victim of lynch mobs.

TUSKEGEE INSTITUTE

. . . .

PLESSY v. FERGUSON

. . . .

WILLIAMS v. MISSISSIPPI

The first formal school for blacks, founded by Booker T. Washington in 1885.

. . . .

This 1896 Supreme Court decision allowed for racial segregation, legalizing "separate but equal" facilities, which was a way of life in the South for nearly 60 years.

. . . .

The 1898 Supreme Court case that upheld the legality of poll taxes and literacy tests, which were designed to deprive blacks of the right to vote.

CHINESE EXCLUSION ACT

. . . .

MUGWUMPS

. . . .

GOLD BUGS

1882 law to effectively end Chinese immigration in response to nativist sentiment that Chinese immigrants—who had come to California in droves during the Gold Rush and built the transcontinental railroad—drove down wages for unskilled labor.

. . . .

A derogatory term for Republican Party activists who objected to their 1884 presidential candidate's corrupt reputation and voted for Democrat Grover Cleveland. Mugwump came to refer to a political figure who deserts his party.

. . . .

Turn-of-the-century term for a supporter of the gold standard for currency (as opposed to the silver standard or currency valuated by the government).

JAMES GILLESPIE BLAINE

. . . .

POPULIST PARTY

. . . .

OMAHA PLATFORM

PART II

Republican presidential candidate in 1884, he lost the election by saying that Irish Catholics were people of "rum, Romanism, and rebellion."

. . . .

Party formed in 1891 to represent the interests of farmers in the South and Midwest. Their agrarian platform opposed the interests of banks, railroads, and corporations. They ran William Jennings Bryan for president in 1896, who the Democrats also endorsed as their candidate.

. . . .

The Populist Party platform for the 1892 election and their candidate James Weaver: national income tax, direct election of senators, railroad regulation, and free coinage of silver.

FREE SILVER

. . . .

PANIC OF 1893

. . . .

JAMES A. GARFIELD

Movement to adopt silver as the basis for American currency that was never adopted because other nations use the gold standard.

. . . .

A severe depression caused by railroad over-speculation and bank runs that left the federal gold supply so low that President Cleveland had to borrow gold from financier J.P. Morgan. Cleveland's Democrats were blamed for the depression, and voters swept in Republican candidates who presided over the Progressive Era.

. . . .

Twentieth president (1881); assassinated shortly after taking office, his civil service reform efforts would be completed by his successor.

HALF-BREEDS

. . . .

POLITICAL MACHINES

. . . .

TAMMANY HALL

Republican political faction of the late 1800s, the party's moderate wing that favored eliminating a patronage system that awarded federal appointments to political allies in favor of a merit-based system. The Half-Breeds, who included President Garfield and Maine senator James G. Blaine, passed the Pendleton Civil Service Reform Act in 1883.

. . . .

Political organizations led by a party boss or group that commands enough votes (often through graft and intimidation) to hold political and administrative control in a city or state. One of the most famous in American history is New York's Tammany Hall.

. . . .

Democratic political machine controlling New York City politics for much of the late 1800s and early 1900s. Tammany had wide (and often corrupting) influence in city political nominations, public contracts, and jobs, earning political capital through popularity among immigrants, especially the Irish.

STALWARTS

. . . .

CHESTER A. ARTHUR

. . . .

CREDIT MOBILIER

Republicans during the late 1800s who favored a machine-politics system of patronage for federal appointments, thereby awarding government jobs to supporters, as opposed to a merit-based system for these positions.

. . . .

Twenty-first president (1881–1885); Republicans passed the Pendleton Civil Service Reform Act despite his alliance with pro-patronage. Arthur's predecessor, President James A. Garfield, had been assassinated by a deranged office seeker.

. . . .

Stockholders of the Union Pacific Railroad owned this construction company and used it to charge the federal government twice the actual cost of the work. When the scheme was discovered, the company tried to bribe government officials to stop the investigation.

GROVER CLEVELAND

PART II

. . . .

WILLIAM JENNINGS BRYAN

. . . .

GOLD STANDARD ACT

The only president to serve nonconsecutive terms, he was the 22nd and 24th president (1885–1889 and 1893–1897). A principled reformer who battled corruption and patronage, his second presidency was undone by the Panic of 1893 and the resulting political divide in his own Democratic Party. Cleveland intervened in the Pullman Strike and strongly favored the gold standard.

· ·

A repeat Democratic candidate for president, Bryan was an ardent opponent of the gold standard. A deeply religious man, he served as prosecutor in the Scopes Monkey Trial.

· ·

This 1900 act held that American paper currency would be backed only by gold. Silver coinage was eliminated and the government was forced to hold gold reserves to exchange for paper currency.

ALEXANDER GRAHAM BELL

. . . .

THOMAS EDISON

. . . .

WOMEN'S CHRISTIAN
TEMPERANCE UNION

PART II

Invented the telephone in 1876.

. . . .

A prolific inventor, Edison created or developed practical versions of the electric light bulb, the phonograph, the mimeograph, and other innovations of the modern electrical system and telecommunications.

. . . .

A women's organization urging laws against the sale of alcohol and promoting total abstinence.

GRANGER MOVEMENT

. . . .

GILDED AGE

. . . .

CHARLES DARWIN

PART II

Agrarian organizations seeking political and economic power for farmers, they opposed corrupt business practices and monopolies. Small grange organizations eventually combined with labor unions to form the Progressive Party.

. . . .

Term for the late 1800s due to the rapid growth of industrial wealth and the luxurious lifestyles of the new captains of industry. The phrase, coined by Mark Twain, was ironic in that economic progress masked widespread poverty and corruption.

. . . .

British scientist whose theory of evolution caused an uproar for suggesting that people and animals were not created but simply part of an ongoing natural process of mutation and adaptation.

SOCIAL DARWINISM

. . . .

BESSEMER PROCESS

. . . .

LAISSEZ-FAIRE ECONOMICS

Darwin's "survival of the fittest" concept came to be used in the 1870s to defend social or political policies that didn't favor disadvantaged people or businesses. The ideology fell out of favor when it was adopted to justify imperialism and theories of racial inferiority.

· ·

A process refined in 1855 to make possible the mass production of steel that enabled the construction of large steel structures like skyscrapers.

· ·

This concept postulates that an economy thrives when government does not regulate business.

NOUVEAU RICHE

. . . .

ROBBER BARONS

. . . .

JOHN D. ROCKEFELLER

PART II

French phrase meaning "new rich" used to distinguish those who became wealthy through industry from those whose family wealth spanned generations.

. . . .

Popular name for big business owners who got rich by swindling the government or forming illegal business combinations.

. . . .

Owner of the Standard Oil Company and one of the nation's wealthiest and most powerful businessmen.

ANDREW CARNEGIE

. . . .

CORNELIUS VANDERBILT

. . . .

GUSTAVUS SWIFT

PART
II

Steel industry magnate and philanthropist.

. . . .

Controlled the New York Central railroad; a powerful and influential businessman.

. . . .

Meat industry magnate who grew to power with the development of refrigerated railcars for transporting meat and the industrial uses of many meat by-products.

AP* U.S. HISTORY FLASH REVIEW

NATIONAL LABOR UNION

KNIGHTS OF LABOR

COLLECTIVE BARGAINING

The first national labor federation founded in 1866 and responsible for the eight-hour workday. The NLU dissolved quickly but laid the foundation for more successful labor federations.

. . . .

Unlike other labor organizations, the Knights survived the depression of the 1870s. They used increasingly radical measures to advocate for equal pay for men and women, laws against child labor, and sanitation and safety requirements in the workplace.

. . . .

A demand of labor unions, collective bargaining is the right of laborers to negotiate hours, wages, and labor conditions with employers.

AP* U.S. HISTORY FLASH REVIEW

YELLOW DOG CONTRACT

. . . .

AMERICAN FEDERATION
OF LABOR

. . . .

SAMUEL GOMPERS

A contract between labor and management by which workers agree not to join unions while they work for a particular company.

. . . .

Largest federation of labor unions in the nation for decades after its inception, the AFL was less radical than other federations.

. . . .

Founder of the American Federation of Labor in 1886, Gompers united unions and encouraged them to elect supportive political candidates.

HAYMARKET SQUARE RIOT

. . . .

PINKERTONS

. . . .

MOTHER JONES

After Chicago police shot laborers protesting for a shorter workday in 1886, over 100,000 rallied in the city's Haymarket Square. During the rally, a German immigrant detonated a bomb that killed a policeman. The event (and the trial that followed) stirred xenophobia.

· ·

A select squad of Chicago policemen often used to disrupt strikes.

· ·

A labor organizer who brought the issues of child labor and unequal pay for women to the attention of political leaders; also a founder of the Industrial Workers of the World.

HORATIO ALGER

. . . .

PULLMAN STRIKE

. . . .

SHERMAN ANTITRUST ACT

Gilded Age author who wrote rags-to-riches tales of poor young men who find success through hard work and perseverance. These stories defined the American dream for generations to come.

· ·

Strike of railroad employees in 1894. Socialist leader Eugene Debs led a labor boycott of Pullman railcars. The protests turned violent, and President Cleveland declared the strike was illegal according to the Sherman Act, as it disrupted mail delivery.

· ·

Enacted in 1890, the first federal antitrust act. It opposed monopolies and other corporate combinations that constrain trade or competition. Later amended by the Clayton Act.

TRUST

· ·

HORIZONTAL CONSOLIDATION

· ·

VERTICAL CONSOLIDATION

A combination of two or more companies in the same industry for the purpose of reducing competition and controlling prices.

. . . .

A type of monopoly that occurs when a company controls one aspect of a manufacturing process.

. . . .

A type of monopoly occurring when a company controls every step of the manufacturing process for a particular product, including raw materials, suppliers, and distribution.

UNITED STATES v. E.C. KNIGHT COMPANY

. . . .

BENJAMIN HARRISON

. . . .

LILIUOKALANI

The Supreme Court decided in 1895 that a sugar company's monopoly had no direct effect on commerce and thus couldn't be regulated by the government.

. . . .

Twenty-third president (1889–1893); grandson of William Henry Harrison; passed the landmark Sherman Antitrust Act and the protectionist McKinley Tariff.

. . . .

Queen of Hawaii deposed by American forces in 1893. The island kingdom become first a protectorate and eventually an American state, as Hawaii offered a valuable naval outpost in the Pacific.

BOXER REBELLION

PART II

. . . .

OPEN DOOR POLICY

. . . .

WILLIAM MCKINLEY

The Boxer Rebellion of the 1890s was started by Chinese nationalists opposed to Western imperialism and the presence of Christian missionaries in China. The group massacred thousands of foreigners and Chinese who converted to Christianity. It took armies from the United States, Great Britain, France, Italy, and Japan to stop the rebellion, which came to a halt in August 1900.

. . . .

Secretary of State John Hull's phrase for equal trade among imperialist nations trading in China.

. . . .

Twenty-fifth president (1897–1901); presided over rapid economic growth and America's first imperialist venture after the Spanish-American War; he also annexed Hawaii. McKinley was assassinated shortly after beginning his second term by the anarchist Leon Czolgosz.

JOSEPH PULITZER

. . . .

WILLIAM RANDOLPH HEARST

. . . .

USS *MAINE*

Publisher of the *New York World* newspaper, he changed American journalism by publishing human-interest stories, scandal, and sensationalism to compete for readers with William Randolph Hearst. He crusaded against corporate greed and corruption.

· ·

Powerful newspaper magnate whose political influence was said to have rallied support for the Spanish-American War.

· ·

Battleship sunk in Havana harbor under mysterious circumstances. Still, inflammatory newspapers blamed Spain, and the *Maine*'s sinking precipitated the Spanish-American War.

JINGOISM

. . . .

IMPERIALISM

. . . .

YELLOW JOURNALISM

A form of extreme nationalism that advocates the use of threats or military force against foreign countries to protect national interests.

. . . .

Describes a powerful nation conquering or controlling a weaker nation's politics and economy.

. . . .

The style of late nineteenth- and early twentieth-century journalists and newspapers who used sensationalistic headlines to grab attention. Stories were often untrue or biased in a way to influence the reading audience at a time when newspapers were the only source of information.

SPANISH-AMERICAN WAR

. . . .

ROUGH RIDERS

. . . .

TREATY OF PARIS

PART II

War between Spain and the United States in 1898 stemming from Cuba's war for independence. The belligerents fought on another front in the Philippines. The conflict ultimately led to American victory and possession of former Spanish colonies Guam, Cuba, the Philippines, and Puerto Rico.

• •

This volunteer battalion recruited by Theodore Roosevelt made him famous after they won a key 1898 battle against Spain at San Juan Hill in Santiago, Cuba.

• •

Ended the Spanish-American War in 1898 and awarded the territories of Guam, Cuba, Puerto Rico, and the Philippines to the United States.

PROTECTORATE

. . . .

PHILIPPINE INSURRECTION

. . . .

PORTSMOUTH TREATY

A small country under the protection of a more powerful nation, such as Cuba to the United States after the Spanish-American War.

• •

A Filipino rebellion against U.S. colonization beginning in 1899. This conflict is also known for guerilla warfare, a tactic of the Filipinos.

• •

Document signed by the Russians and Japanese that ended the Russo-Japanese War in 1905. For negotiating the treaty, President Theodore Roosevelt won the Nobel Peace Prize.

HAY-PAUNCEFOTE TREATY

. . . .

PANAMA CANAL

. . . .

THEODORE ROOSEVELT

Signed by the United States and United Kingdom in 1901, this agreement stated that the United States would have sole rights in constructing and controlling the Panama Canal. Both countries later agreed that such a canal should not be controlled by just one nation.

• •

Roughly 50 miles in length, the Panama Canal was constructed by the United States between 1904 and 1914. It allowed faster access between the Atlantic and Pacific, and continues to be an important conduit for international trade and travel.

• •

Twenty-sixth president (1901–1909); icon of the Progressive Era; promised "a Square Deal" for Americans and delivered by breaking up trusts and pushing for social reforms. His robust foreign policy included pushing for the Panama Canal and negotiating an end to the Russo-Japanese War.

AP* U.S. HISTORY FLASH REVIEW

ROOSEVELT COROLLARY

. . . .

BIG STICK POLICY

. . . .

NORTHERN SECURITIES
COMPANY

PART
II

In an attempt to block further European expansion into the Western Hemisphere, this corollary to the Monroe Doctrine stated that the United States might intervene if a Latin American country was experiencing large debts or civil unrest.

. . . .

President Theodore Roosevelt said of his foreign policy, "speak softly and carry a big stick." This political ideology was more about intimidation than actual military force.

. . . .

A railroad trust formed in 1902. Theodore Roosevelt sued the company according to the Sherman Antitrust Act for creating a monopoly. The Supreme Court ruled against the company, which was dissolved, a major victory for Roosevelt and antitrust activists.

PROGRESSIVE ERA

. . . .

MUCKRAKERS

. . . .

JANE ADDAMS

An era of social activism and political reform from the 1890s to the 1920s. Reformers at the national and local levels attempted to end corporate and government corruption and solve social ills such as alcoholism, poverty, and illiteracy. The movement involved women to a greater extent than previous political eras.

· ·

A term used to describe Progressive Era investigative journalists who wrote exposés on economic and political corruption, as well as social problems in an increasingly industrial society.

· ·

Social reformer for the working class, she opened Chicago's Hull House, the nation's first private social welfare organization.

TENEMENTS

· ·

SECOND WAVE OF
IMMIGRATION

· ·

SOCIAL GOSPEL MOVEMENT

PART
II

Urban housing for factory laborers (later for immigrants), often overcrowded and poorly constructed.

. . . .

Second wave of immigrants from Eastern and Southern Europe, including many Jews and Italians, from 1865 to 1910.

. . . .

A turn-of-the-century movement that promoted social responsibility as a means of spiritual salvation.

PART II

FUNDAMENTALISTS

. . . .

MARGARET SANGER

. . . .

FRANK LLOYD WRIGHT

Refers to a broad Protestant movement to defend Christian ideals from more liberal religious philosophies or secularism. Some fundamentalist theologies hold that the Bible is the literal truth.

. . . .

After serving as a nurse in New York slums, Sanger saw the suffering caused by unwanted pregnancy. She led the movement to legalize birth control and opened the nation's first birth control clinic.

. . . .

America's greatest architect, he designed not only notable public buildings like New York's Guggenheim museum, but also revolutionized the design and layout of the American home.

TRIANGLE SHIRTWAIST
COMPANY FIRE

. . . .

UPTON SINCLAIR

. . . .

PURE FOOD AND DRUG ACT

PART II

A 1911 fire in a New York City factory that killed 146 people (mostly women) due to unsafe working conditions. The tragedy led to federal acts to protect workers.

. . . .

Writer best known for his 1906 muckraking novel, *The Jungle*, which exposed unsanitary conditions in the Chicago meat-packing industry. His work led to a federal investigation under President Roosevelt and eventually, the 1906 Pure Food and Drug Act.

. . . .

Enacted in 1906 by the federal government to protect the American consumer, the law provided for mandated inspection of meat products. It also sought to stop the mislabeling of "quack medicines," pharmaceuticals promoted as healthful that had no scientific evidence to back up advertised claims.

JACOB RIIS

. . . .

IDA TARBELL

. . . .

EUGENE DEBS

Muckraking photojournalist best known for his 1890 book *How the Other Half Lives*, which documented and exposed the difficult lives and squalid living conditions of the impoverished lower-class living in the slums of New York City.

. . . .

Muckraking female journalist who wrote for McClure's magazine. She is best known for her exposé "The History of the Standard Oil Company" (1904).

. . . .

Socialist Party candidate in the 1908 and 1912 elections, Debs was imprisoned according to the Sedition Act during World War I.

NIAGARA MOVEMENT

. . . .

NATIONAL ASSOCIATION FOR THE ADVANCEMENT OF COLORED PEOPLE (NAACP)

. . . .

BULL MOOSE PARTY

African-American civil rights organization that met near Niagara Falls, NY in 1905 to author a Declaration of Principles. These included racial equality, women's suffrage, and full civil liberties for black Americans. Later absorbed into the NAACP.

. . . .

A civil rights organization founded in 1909 to preserve equality for African Americans and eliminate racism. The NAACP was a driving force to overturn Jim Crow laws.

. . . .

Nickname for the Progressive Party, which ran Theodore Roosevelt for president in the election of 1912. Roosevelt's third party was so popular that he split the Republican vote, which allowed Woodrow Wilson to win the election.

NEW NATIONALISM

. . . .

WILLIAM HOWARD TAFT

. . . .

DOLLAR DIPLOMACY

PART
II

Theodore Roosevelt's 1912 Progressive party platform, this plan endorsed a more active social and economic role for government, continued antitrust regulation, and women's suffrage and social welfare programs.

· ·

Twenty-seventh president (1909–1913); trust-busting Republican who passed the first federal income tax law.

· ·

Refers to the United States guaranteeing loans made to Latin American countries to maintain stable governments and protect American interests in the region. The practice is part of the Roosevelt Corollary, allowing the United States to intervene if neighboring nations seem economically vulnerable to European creditors.

SIXTEENTH AMENDMENT

. . . .

CLAYTON ANTITRUST ACT

. . . .

FEDERAL RESERVE ACT

Ratified in 1913, it allowed Congress to collect income taxes. Very much a product of the Progressive Era, income taxes shifted more of the tax burden to the wealthy.

• •

The Clayton Antitrust Act of 1914 added to the scope of the Sherman Antitrust Act of 1890. Individuals from one company were no longer allowed to have a directorship on the board of a competing company. In addition, changes were made to laws on mergers & acquisitions. Companies were not allowed to merge if the result was a monopoly.

• •

This 1913 act created a banking regulatory agency controlled by the Federal Reserve Board. The Federal Reserve controls money in circulation through reserves and interest rates. In contrast to laissez-faire economics, this act was meant to help small banks stay afloat.

1914–2001

FEDERAL TRADE COMMISSION

. . . .

MONOPOLY

. . . .

LOUIS D. BRANDEIS

PART III

Federal agency established in 1914 to ensure a free consumer marketplace by regulating certain aspects of commerce. It investigates accusations of unfair trade practices and monopolies.

. . . .

When a specific person or company exclusively controls a particular commodity. As a result of having total control of the market, the company can manipulate and control pricing, which can negatively impact the economy and competitive marketplace.

. . . .

Attorney who pushed for banking reform and laws protecting women in the workplace, Brandeis was nominated for the Supreme Court in 1916 and became the first Jewish American to serve as a justice.

WOODROW WILSON

. . . .

NEW FREEDOM

. . . .

ZIMMERMAN NOTE

Twenty-eighth president (1913–1921); prolific Progressive domestic agenda included the Clayton Antitrust Act and creating the Federal Trade Commission and Federal Reserve. He also advocated for women's suffrage and against child labor, led the nation into World War I, and his Fourteen Points were a postwar vision for a world without war.

. . . .

Wilson's political platform advancing entrepreneurship and markets with few regulations but no monopolies.

. . . .

A major impetus for the United States to enter World War I, this secret telegram written by the German foreign secretary was discovered to contain a proposed German-Mexican alliance in the coming global conflict with promises for Mexico to regain American land in the Southwest.

LUSITANIA

. . . .

WORLD WAR I

PART III

. . . .

REPARATIONS

A British transatlantic liner torpedoed by the Germans on May 7, 1915. Over 1,000 people died. This unprovoked attack is considered to be the strongest contributing factor for the United States to enter World War I.

. . . .

When the territorial ambitions of Europe's empires exploded into war, the entire continent was drawn into the conflict via alliances—the United Kingdom, France and Russia versus Germany, Austria-Hungary and Italy. The Great War, as it came to be known, took over nine million lives through gruesome trench warfare and new mechanized weapons. The result was a new Europe: the end of empires in Germany, Russia, Austria-Hungary, and Turkey.

. . . .

Payments or services provided by a perpetrator to a victim to account for property damage or other loss. After World War I, the victors forced Germany to accept responsibility for the war and pay reparations to its opponents.

TREATY OF VERSAILLES

. . . .

FOURTEEN POINTS

. . . .

LEAGUE OF NATIONS

This treaty ended World War I though it did little to change the prewar power structure in Europe or prevent future conflict. Within decades, the treaty was widely ridiculed for ineffectiveness and creating conditions in Germany that may have encouraged the rise of Nazism.

. . . .

President Wilson's World War I peace plan designed to prevent future conflicts, which included free trade, open peace treaties, and a world government. Wilson was forced to compromise each point at the Paris Peace Conference except for the founding of a League of Nations.

. . . .

President Wilson's vision for an intergovernmental organization came to reality after World War I. Dedicated to maintaining world peace, the League dissolved in the 1930s when it failed to prevent fascist powers in Europe from attacking their neighbors.

AP* U.S. HISTORY FLASH REVIEW

UNITED STATES REFUSES LEAGUE OF NATIONS

. . . .

U-BOATS

. . . .

BOLSHEVIKS

PART III

Congress voted against joining the League
of Nations, claiming the League would limit
American self-determinism, including the right
of Congress to declare war.

. . . .

German submarines used in World War I and
World War II to attack other military vessels,
supply ships, and even civilian boats for the
purpose of intimidation.

. . . .

Russian socialists led by Lenin in 1917 who
organized a revolution to overthrow the tsar.
They became a symbol of the possibilities of
socialist revolution around the world.

BLACK MIGRATION TO THE NORTH

. . . .

MARCUS GARVEY

. . . .

HARLEM RENAISSANCE

PART III

Due to increased industrial jobs to support the war and the growth of northern factories, blacks left the South in droves during World War I to seek better economic opportunities.

. . . .

Radical black leader who proclaimed that blacks would get no justice in white nations and urged his people to move back to Africa.

. . . .

During the first half of the 1900s, Harlem became a center for black writers, musicians, and intellectuals, from jazz musicians like Duke Ellington to writers like Langston Hughes.

PROPAGANDA

. . . .

ESPIONAGE AND SEDITION
ACTS

. . . .

FIRST RED SCARE

PART
III

Mass-marketed messages intended to influence public thought. The United States engaged in propaganda in World War I, for example, to rally popular support for the war.

. . . .

To spurn nationalism and maintain support for America's involvement in World War I, these acts were largely used to prosecute antiwar socialists and radical labor union members.

. . . .

Widespread fear during the 1920s that communism would come to the United States. Businesses exploited this fear in order to control labor unions.

PALMER RAIDS

. . . .

SACCO AND VANZETTI

. . . .

KU KLUX KLAN

PART III

Red Scare crackdown on suspected communists in 1919 and 1920 resulting in hundreds of
arrests, mainly targeting immigrants.

. . . .

Two Italian immigrants convicted of murder
on flimsy evidence in 1927 and sentenced to
death. Xenophobia (fear of foreigners) may
have played a role in their conviction, as well
as their alleged affiliation with anarchist and
union organizations.

. . . .

A racist organization that grew in the 1920s,
the Klan threatened violence toward anyone
in the United States who was not from a white,
Protestant background.

HENRY CABOT LODGE

. . . .

EMERGENCY QUOTA ACT
OF 1921

. . . .

IMMIGRATION QUOTA ACT
OF 1924

PART
III

An outspoken Massachusetts senator who introduced a bill to limit immigration through literacy tests. Lodge also led Republicans against American involvement in the League of Nations.

· ·

This act limited immigration to 3% of each nationality already within the United States according to the 1910 census.

· ·

This act reduced quotas for immigration from 3% to 2% of the total U.S. population for that nationality in order to preserve the country's racial composition.

ROBERT LA FOLLETTE

. . . .

F. SCOTT FITZGERALD

. . . .

EIGHTEENTH AMENDMENT

PART III

Wisconsin senator and 1924 Progressive Party presidential candidate who called for government ownership of the railroads and relief for farmers.

. . . .

Author of *The Great Gatsby*, which depicts American society's increasing glorification of wealth and achievement.

. . . .

Outlawed the manufacture and sale of "intoxicating liquors." It was ratified in 1919, though the Volstead Act, which enforced the amendment, did not begin until 1920. The Twenty-First Amendment repealed the Eighteenth Amendment in 1933. This is the only amendment to be repealed in its entirety.

PROHIBITION

. . . .

VOLSTEAD ACT

. . . .

NINETEENTH AMENDMENT

PART III

Prohibition was a federal ban on the manufacture and sale of alcohol from 1920 through 1933.

. . . .

Also known as the National Prohibition Act, the Volstead Act was written to provide enforcement of the Eighteenth Amendment to the Constitution, which had begun the period of U.S. Prohibition.

. . . .

Ratified in 1920, this amendment gave women the right to vote.

FLAPPERS

. . . .

JOHN T. SCOPES

. . . .

CLARENCE DARROW

PART III

A term for young women of the 1920s who many considered to be immodest for their fast lifestyles and bold new fashions such as short skirts and bobbed hairstyles.

. . . .

Defendant in the 1925 trial centered on teaching evolution. Scopes was indicted for teaching Darwin's theory in Tennessee. Though he was convicted and had to pay a petty fine, Clarence Darrow's sharp-witted defense of Scopes made his fundamentalist accusers look foolish.

. . . .

The famed criminal defense lawyer at "the Scopes Monkey Trial" whose clever defense of evolution embarrassed William Jennings Bryan, considered to be one of the great American orators.

THE JAZZ SINGER

. . . .

CHARLES LINDBERGH

. . . .

HENRY FORD

The first motion picture with sound in 1927, it starred Al Jolson, a white man, portraying a black jazz singer.

. . . .

Lindbergh became a national hero in 1927 when he became the first person to fly solo across the Atlantic Ocean. A staunch isolationist, he was a notable public voice against the United States entering World War II.

. . . .

Revolutionized the auto industry through assembly line manufacturing and made cars affordable for many Americans.

WARREN G. HARDING

. . . .

CALVIN COOLIDGE

. . . .

TEAPOT DOME SCANDAL

PART
III

Twenty-ninth president (1921–1923); remembered less for economic success during his presidency than scandals and corruption in his administration, including the Teapot Dome Scandal. Died in office.

. . . .

Thirtieth president (1923–1929); presided over economic growth and general prosperity and reduced the size of the federal government.

. . . .

Several Cabinet members were forced to resign in 1929 when it was discovered they had taken bribes from oil companies to manage the naval oil reserves.

HERBERT HOOVER

. . . .

BLACK TUESDAY

. . . .

HOOVERVILLE

PART III

Thirty-first president (1929–1933). The stock market crashed only weeks into his presidency, and Hoover is remembered as being unable to prevent the Great Depression, though some of his early efforts (including public works projects like Hoover Dam) inspired New Deal programs.

. . . .

The largest stock market crash in American history, on October 29, 1929, that began the Great Depression.

. . . .

Ironic name for the shantytowns created on vacant lots and public land during the Depression, which reflected widespread blame for Hoover's inaction or ineffectiveness to heal the economy.

SMOOT–HAWLEY TARIFF ACT

. . . .

TWENTY-FIRST AMENDMENT

. . . .

FRANKLIN D. ROOSEVELT

PART
III

A 1930 act that raised the tariff on imported agricultural and industrial goods that some say exacerbated the Depression.

. . . .

Ended Prohibition in 1933 after a government commission determined that banning alcohol had actually led to an increase in crime.

. . . .

Thirty-second president (1933–1945); only president elected to four terms; led America through the Depression with the New Deal programs that extended the reach of the federal government to address the crisis; also led the nation during World War II.

GREAT DEPRESSION

....

BONUS ARMY

....

DUST BOWL

PART
III

A combination of economic factors led to the crash: In the United States, inflated stock prices, excessive debt, and industrial overproduction; in Europe, when Germany defaulted on World War I reparations, several European banks failed.

. . . .

Veterans of World War I hit hard by the Depression who marched on Washington to demand aid to alleviate their economic suffering.

. . . .

Term for the drought-afflicted prairie territory in the Southeast during the Depression. Many Texas and Oklahoma farmers abandoned their land and traveled west in search of new opportunities.

NEW DEAL

. . . .

NEW DEAL COALITION

. . . .

JOHN MAYNARD KEYNES

PART III

Franklin Roosevelt's plan to heal the economy focused on relief, recovery, and reform. Roosevelt pushed through programs to increase employment, increase the minimum wage, and reform many other social issues.

. . . .

Roosevelt united factions of voters who seldom agreed, creating a broad base of support for his New Deal among ethnic minorities, southern whites, and organized labor.

. . . .

British economist who believed that increasing government spending could pull an economy out of depression by creating jobs and empowering consumers. These theories were the basis for FDR's economic programs.

BANK RUN

· ·

GLASS-STEAGALL ACT

PART III

· ·

BANK HOLIDAY

Occurs when citizens or investors withdraw substantial amounts from banks to hold their money privately or exchange currency for gold; a major cause of several economic panics, including the Great Depression.

. . . .

This 1933 act allowed defaulted banks to reopen and gave the government power to regulate banking transactions and foreign exchange. The act created the Federal Deposit Insurance Corporation, which insures the accounts of depositors of its member banks. The act also outlawed banks investing in the stock market.

. . . .

To slow the tide of bank failures, FDR instituted a bank holiday in March 1933. As all banks were closed, people could not remove their savings and force banks to shut down for lack of deposits.

EMERGENCY BANKING RELIEF ACT

. . . .

TENNESSEE VALLEY AUTHORITY (TVA)

. . . .

NATIONAL LABOR RELATIONS BOARD

PART III

This 1933 act instituted a forced bank holiday and instituted government oversight of poorly managed banks, which helped to restore public confidence in the banks.

. . . .

FDR founded this government-owned corporation to create jobs supplying electricity to poor rural areas.

. . . .

An administrative board that gave laborers the rights of self-organization and collective bargaining.

CIVILIAN CONSERVATION
CORPS (CCC)

. . . .

FEDERAL HOUSING AUTHORITY

. . . .

SECOND NEW DEAL

PART
III

The CCC provided employment during the Great Depression, including projects in reforestation, flood control, and draining swamplands.

. . . .

President Franklin Roosevelt created this agency to provide sanitary and low-cost housing for the poor during the Great Depression.

. . . .

The second stage beginning in 1935 of Franklin Roosevelt's plan to pull the nation out of the Depression, this included the Social Security Act.

SOCIAL SECURITY ACT OF 1935

. . . .

WORKS PROGRESS
ADMINISTRATION (WPA)

. . . .

REVENUE ACT

Created a federal insurance program funded by taxes from employees' wages. Workers would receive money from this fund as a monthly pension when they reached the age of 65. These funds would also go to the unemployed, disabled, and unwed or widowed mothers with dependent children.

. . . .

New Deal agency created in 1935 to create jobs by hiring men to work on bridges, roads, and buildings. Almost 9 million men were hired.

. . . .

This 1935 act absorbed up to 75% of incomes over $5 million and also levied high taxes on large gifts, inheritances, and capital gains—hence its nickname, "the soak the rich tax."

GOOD NEIGHBOR POLICY

. . . .

FATHER COUGHLIN

. . . .

FASCISM

PART III

FDR's Latin American policy, which refuted the first Roosevelt Corollary: The United States will not intervene in the domestic affairs of Latin America, instead serving as a reciprocal partner in trade and strategic alliances.

• •

Catholic priest who was one of the loudest opponents of the New Deal. His radio program was canceled in 1942 when it became too radical.

• •

An authoritarian nationalist political ideology. Fascism preaches that a nation or civilization is superior and unites the people around a totalitarian state that purges dissenting ideas. Germany's Nazi Party, Benito Mussolini in Italy, and Spain's Francisco Franco were fascists who came to power during the 1920s and 1930s.

HITLER-STALIN NONAGGRESSION PACT

. . . .

NAZI PARTY

. . . .

GERMAN INVASION OF POLAND

PART
III

A 1939 pact between Hitler and Stalin that allowed Germany to attack Poland without Russian retaliation.

. . . .

A fascist political organization in Germany led by Adolf Hitler, the Nazis upheld a strong central government with absolute power. The Nazis believed that the needs of the state outweighed those of individuals and also upheld a racist ideology that non-Aryan people (especially Jews) were inferior to Germans.

. . . .

The impetus for Great Britain and France to declare war on Germany in 1939.

AXIS POWERS

. . . .

THE HOLOCAUST

. . . .

VICHY GOVERNMENT

PART III

The coalition formed by Italy, Germany, and Japan during World War II.

. . . .

Hitler's "final solution" for the Jews and other non-Aryan peoples was relocation to extermination camps throughout Europe, where over 12 million noncombatants were murdered.

. . . .

The puppet French government arranged by the Nazis after they conquered France in 1941.

AMERICA FIRST COMMITTEE

. . . .

ATLANTIC CHARTER

. . . .

LEND-LEASE LAW

An isolationist committee to prevent American involvement in World War II. Its most prominent figure was the aviator Charles Lindbergh.

. . . .

A secret 1941 meeting between Winston Churchill and President Franklin D. Roosevelt outlined their vision for a postwar world: self-government, free trade, and no territorial changes.

. . . .

A 1941 law allowing the United States to lend or lease weapons to foreign victims of aggression, which helped American allies but kept the country from active fighting.

ISOLATIONISM

. . . .

NEUTRALITY ACTS

. . . .

"CASH AND CARRY"

PART III

Political belief that the United States should not involve itself in foreign affairs, a sentiment that grew especially strong before both world wars.

. . . .

These acts were intended to create restrictions to keep the United States out of foreign wars. Americans were not allowed to travel on a ship belonging to a belligerent nation nor make loans or sell munitions to a belligerent nation. The acts were not passed.

. . . .

Refers to a policy restricting the sale of American munitions to European allies. Britain and France would have to pay for weapons in cash and transport them on their own ships.

PEARL HARBOR

. . . .

INTERNMENT CAMPS

. . . .

WAR PRODUCTION BOARD

PART III

Site of the surprise Japanese air attack on the U.S. Pacific fleet in Hawaii on December 7, 1941. The United States declared war on Japan the next day.

· ·

Government-run camps where Japanese-Americans were relocated to prevent espionage during World War II.

· ·

Halted the manufacture of nonessential items during World War II in order to preserve resources and raw materials for the war effort. The board also reconfigured factories for military manufacturing.

JOSEPH STALIN

. . . .

STALINGRAD

. . . .

D-DAY

PART III

Soviet premier from 1922 to 1953. Responsible for rapid industrialization, brutal repression of political opponents, and forced relocation of millions of workers.

. . . .

The first major loss for Germany during World War II, where Russian forces repelled the German army's eastward advance into the USSR in 1942.

. . . .

D-Day was the date of the marine invasion of Western Europe when a massive armada of U.S. and British forces landed in France on June 6, 1944.

BATTLE OF THE BULGE

. . . .

V-E DAY

. . . .

YALTA CONFERENCE

PART III

A turning point in the European campaign, Allied Forces held off a massive German attack during the winter of 1944–1945 and retained their position at the German border.

. . . .

May 7, 1945, when Germany surrendered to the Allies: Victory in Europe Day.

. . . .

A February 1945 meeting of Allied leaders to discuss conditions for ending the war against Germany and postwar divisions of power in Europe.

POTSDAM CONFERENCE

. . . .

ISLAND-HOPPING

. . . .

OKINAWA

PART
III

At this August 1945 summit in Germany between President Truman, Stalin, and British prime minister Clement Attlee, the Allies warned Japan they must surrender unconditionally.

. . . .

Starting in Australia, the United States conquered Pacific islands one by one to get closer to Japan for the final invasion, which never occurred—the United States chose instead to drop two atomic bombs to force Japanese surrender.

. . . .

Island only 300 miles from Japan, site of a bloody turning point in the Pacific campaign. Over two months in 1945, over 50,000 Americans and 100,000 Japanese died battling for control of Okinawa, finally won by the United States in June.

MANHATTAN PROJECT

. . . .

ROBERT OPPENHEIMER

. . . .

HIROSHIMA AND NAGASAKI

PART III

The secretive American project to design an atomic warhead to be used against Germany or Japan during World War II.

. . . .

A physics professor and key member of the Manhattan Project, he was later deposed from his seat on the Atomic Energy Commission under suspicions that he was a Communist.

. . . .

Japanese cities destroyed by atomic bombs in August 1945 that led to the deaths of over 200,000 civilians by some estimates. The bombings forced Japan to surrender.

HARRY S TRUMAN

. . . .

V-J DAY

. . . .

NUREMBERG TRIALS

Thirty-third president (1945–1953); made the decision to drop atomic bombs on Japan, effectively ending the war. The Truman Doctrine, advocating containment of communism, is considered the basis of Cold War political policy and the rationale behind both the Korean War and Vietnam.

· ·

August 15, 1945, when Japan surrendered after the United States dropped atomic bombs on Hiroshima and Nagasaki: Victory in Japan Day.

· ·

To punish Nazi leaders after World War II and ensure no other fascists would attempt to seize power in Germany, the Allies tried 22 Nazi war criminals in Nuremberg, Germany in 1945 and 1946. Most were executed or jailed.

JACKIE ROBINSON

. . . .

ISRAEL

PART
III

. . . .

FAIR DEAL

First African-American baseball player allowed to play in baseball's major leagues. Prior to 1947, the sport was segregated and African-American players were relegated to the Negro Leagues.

. . . .

Jewish state established in the former British Mandate of Palestine in 1948. Israel became an important American ally as a democracy among Middle Eastern dictatorships, yet the alliance also strained American relationships with Israel's neighbors.

. . . .

President Truman's domestic policy guaranteeing jobs to soldiers returning from World War II, raising the minimum wage and bolstering Social Security.

BABY BOOM

. . . .

G.I. BILL

. . . .

COLD WAR

PART
III

Thanks to the end of the Depression, postwar prosperity, and new economic mobility, the American birth rate soared from 1945 to 1957. The generation born during the era is known as the baby boomers.

. . . .

Also known as the Servicemen's Readjustment Act of 1944, the bill afforded monetary benefits to returning veterans, including payment of college tuition, low-cost mortgages, and loans to start a business.

. . . .

A period of indirect hostility between the United States and the Soviet Union from roughly the end of World War II until 1991. Largely an ideological conflict between capitalism and communism, the American effort to contain or repel the spread of communist influence inspired wars in Korea and Vietnam and numerous minor military engagements and standoffs.

TRUMAN DOCTRINE

. . . .

NATIONAL SECURITY ACT

. . . .

MARSHALL PLAN

PART III

This 1947 doctrine outlines Truman's foreign policy and is the basis for America's Cold War policy. While formally promising assistance to democratic governments in Greece and Turkey, it promised support to any country threatened by communist revolutions. Truman's containment strategy was the basis for the Korean and Vietnam wars.

· ·

This 1947 act replaced the War Department and in its place created the Central Intelligence Agency (CIA), the National Security Council, and the Department of Defense.

· ·

Also known as the European Recovery Program (ERP), this policy guaranteed U.S. financial support to European nations rebuilding after World War II. By strengthening their economies and infrastructures, the United States would halt the spread of communism by preventing revolutions in war-torn Europe.

BERLIN WALL

. . . .

BERLIN AIRLIFT

SUPERPOWERS

. . . .

Communist forces built this wall to prevent citizens from fleeing East Germany into the American-controlled portion of the city, an enclave of democratic West Germany. The wall remained a symbol of the Cold War until it was dismantled in 1989.

. . . .

A British and American initiative to airlift food and supplies to Soviet-blockaded Berlin in 1948 and 1949 that established American interest in undermining Soviet control in Eastern Europe.

. . . .

After World War II, Europe rebuilt and Asia fought off its colonial rulers, which left the United States and the USSR as the most influential nations.

**NORTH ATLANTIC TREATY
ORGANIZATION (NATO)**

. . . .

SATELLITE STATES

. . . .

WARSAW PACT

PART
III

Military alliance between the United States, Canada, and 10 European nations signed on April 4, 1949, committed to building the military defenses of Europe and threatened the expanding Soviet communism.

· ·

Eastern European countries conquered by Russia during World War II that became Communist-controlled nations with close ties to Moscow after the war: East Germany, Hungary, and Poland.

· ·

In response to NATO, the Warsaw Pact was a strategic alliance of European communist nations and Soviet satellite states in effect until 1991.

IRON CURTAIN

. . . .

TWENTY-SECOND
AMENDMENT

. . . .

HOUSE UN-AMERICAN
ACTIVITIES COMMITTEE

PART
III

Coined by Winston Churchill, the phrase refers to the isolation and secrecy of the Soviet Union and its satellites.

· ·

Ratified by Congress in 1951, this amendment sets a limit of two presidential terms, a measure in direct response to Franklin D. Roosevelt's four consecutive presidencies.

· ·

A committee of the U.S. House of Representatives that investigated alleged communists, most notably during the 1940s when it created a list of suspected Hollywood stars and producers that was largely inaccurate and politically motivated.

JOSEPH McCARTHY

. . . .

McCARTHYISM

. . . .

JULIUS AND ETHEL ROSENBERG

PART III

Wisconsin senator who tried to root out communist infiltration in America. McCarthy's tactics were discredited as many he accused of communist connections were later found to be no threat to national security.

. . . .

The tactics of Wisconsin senator Joseph McCarthy to raise fear of communist infiltration of the American power structure. McCarthy produced a list of names of suspected traitors, most of whom had no connection to communism and posed no threat.

. . . .

American communist sympathizers convicted in 1951 of providing the Soviets with information on U.S. atomic weapons.

MAO TSE-TUNG

· ·

CHIANG KAI-SHEK

PART
III

· ·

**NATIONAL SECURITY COUNCIL
DOCUMENT NSC-68**

Marxist leader of the Communist Party of China who seized control of the country in 1949 and ruled until his death in 1976. His attempts to reorganize the Chinese economy to his Marxist vision is thought to be responsible for the deaths of over 50 million citizens.

• •

Chinese leader deposed by the Communist forces of Mao Tse-Tung in the Chinese revolution of 1949. The United States would not formally recognize the Communist regime, instead referring to Chiang Kai-Shek's exiled party as the true Chinese leadership.

• •

This document, released shortly after China became a communist country in 1949, recommended the use of military force if a country was threatened by communism. This containment strategy was enacted as a crisis in Korea turned into an American war.

ARMS RACE

. . . .

HYDROGEN BOMB

. . . .

KOREAN WAR

PART III

Following the Soviet detonation of an atomic bomb in 1949, both the United States and the Soviet Union engaged in a race to build the world's strongest nuclear weapon and to increase their nuclear arsenals.

• •

The United States detonated the hydrogen bomb (or H-bomb) in 1952. It was more than a thousand times stronger than the bombs dropped on Hiroshima and Nagasaki during World War II.

• •

When communist North Korea, supported by China and the Soviet Union, invaded U.S.-backed South Korea in 1950, war erupted. The two sides fought for three years, neither gaining significant territory, and the war ended in an armistice that created a demilitarized zone at the 38th parallel, which divides the two nations.

DWIGHT D. EISENHOWER

. . . .

GENERAL DOUGLAS MacARTHUR

. . . .

THIRTY-EIGHTH PARALLEL

Thirty-fourth president (1953–1961), known as Ike; Supreme Commander of Allied Expeditionary Forces in western Europe 1943–1945; as president ended the Korean War and aimed to prevent the Soviet Union from expanding its influence by increasing the American nuclear arsenal.

• •

Leader of U.S. military forces in the Pacific theater during World War II, MacArthur oversaw the military occupation and rebuilding of Japan after the war. He later led U.S. forces in the Korean War but was relieved of this duty for questioning U.S. strategy.

• •

The thirty-eighth parallel is the latitudinal line dividing North and South Korea. As part of the armistice that ended the Korean War, the surrounding territory became a demilitarized zone.

EISENHOWER DOCTRINE

. . . .

SHAH OF IRAN

. . . .

NATIONAL INTERSTATE AND DEFENSE HIGHWAYS ACT OF 1956

Similar in ideology to the Truman Doctrine, Eisenhower also promised economic and military assistance to any nation threatened by communism, though Eisenhower's focus included communism in the Middle East.

. . . .

In 1953, the CIA and British intelligence organized a coup d'etat to overthrow the democratically elected prime minister of Iran, giving complete authority to Shah Mohammad Reza Pahlavi, who accommodated the British company that controlled Iran's oil.

. . . .

Another Cold War initiative, this act created the country's interstates. While it improved transportation for the average driver, its primary purpose was to serve as quick, centralized evacuation routes. The highways could also transport missiles and serve as landing strips for airplanes in the event of an emergency.

U-2 INCIDENT

. . . .

AFL-CIO

. . . .

DR. JONAS SALK

The Eisenhower administration was forced to admit that a U-2 spy plane shot down over the Soviet Union in 1960 was taking surveillance photographs. The incident compelled Soviet leader Khrushchev to pull out of an upcoming summit of international leaders.

. . . .

In 1955, rival union federations American Federation of Labor and the Congress of Industrial Organizations merged to form the nation's most powerful labor force.

. . . .

In 1955, Dr. Jonas Salk introduced the polio vaccine, which saved countless lives by virtually ending the paralyzing disease. By the mid-1960s, nearly every child born in the United States received the vaccine.

GENEVA CONFERENCE

. . . .

BROWN v. BOARD OF EDUCATION

. . . .

ROSA PARKS

PART III

The 1954 conference of world powers attempting to unify Vietnam and solve military disputes in the region. Vietnam was divided into two sections along the seventeenth parallel.

• •

The 1954 Supreme Court case in which NAACP lawyer Thurgood Marshall argued that a black student should be allowed to enroll in the same school as white children. The decision in Marshall's favor outlawed separate-but-equal facilities, thus ending legalized segregation.

• •

A pioneer in the civil rights movement, Parks was a black woman arrested in Alabama in 1955 after refusing to give up her bus seat to a white person. Her stance against this racism is considered a motivating factor behind Dr. Martin Luther King, Jr.'s bus boycotts.

AP* U.S. HISTORY FLASH REVIEW

MONTGOMERY BUS BOYCOTTS

. . . .

LITTLE ROCK NINE

. . . .

CIVIL RIGHTS BILL OF 1957

A series of bus boycotts around the country organized by Dr. Martin Luther King, Jr. after the arrest of Rosa Parks. King encouraged blacks to boycott segregated public bus systems. The boycott lasted roughly 400 days and helped to end this form of public segregation.

. . . .

Arkansas Governor Orval Faubus sent the National Guard to prevent nine black students from attending a formerly whites-only Little Rock high school. After a federal court ordered that the students be admitted, violent protests forced President Eisenhower to send federal troops to escort the students into the school.

. . . .

Allowed for the creation of a new department within the Justice Department to monitor civil rights abuses.

CIVIL RIGHTS BILL OF 1960

. . . .

MARTIN LUTHER KING, JR.

. . . .

"I HAVE A DREAM"

PART III

Extending the rights of the Civil Rights Commission, this act allowed the federal government to inspect election sites and fine anyone who interfered with a citizen's ability to vote.

. . . .

Minister and civil rights activist who helped organize the Montgomery bus boycotts and delivered the powerful "I Have a Dream" speech in 1963, which called for racial equality. He was assassinated on April 4, 1968.

. . . .

Iconic speech calling for racial equality delivered by Dr. Martin Luther King, Jr. on August 28, 1963, at the historic march on Washington. King delivered the speech at the National Mall to an audience estimated at 25,000.

FREEDOM RIDERS

. . . .

"BULL" CONNOR

. . . .

GEORGE WALLACE

PART
III

Protest group who dramatized the injustice of segregation on public buses by intentionally seating black and white protesters together in whites-only sections. Violent reaction to these protests, which began in 1961, promoted President Kennedy to further his administration's desegregation efforts.

• •

Public safety chief in Birmingham, Alabama, during the civil rights era who became a symbol of American bigotry. Connor's use of fire hoses and police dogs against peaceful protesters was caught by television cameras and energized the civil rights cause.

• •

Alabama governor who tried to prevent the desegregation of the University of Alabama in 1963. Later a third-party candidate in the 1968 presidential election who ran as an opponent of segregation.

CUBAN REVOLUTION

. . . .

FIDEL CASTRO

. . . .

JOHN F. KENNEDY

Under the leadership of Fidel Castro and his guerilla forces, the government of Fulgencio Batista fell in 1959. Castro became the leader of a new communist government and established an alliance with the Soviet Union.

. . . .

Communist leader of Cuba who assumed leadership in 1959. Castro survived several known American attempts to depose his government, including the failed 1961 Bay of Pigs invasion.

. . . .

Thirty-fifth president (1961–1963); first Catholic president; presided over the failed Bay of Pigs invasion to oust Castro, averted disaster during the Cuban Missile Crisis, promoted American advances in the space race, supported the Civil Rights movement. Assassinated in Dallas in November 1963 by Lee Harvey Oswald.

BAY OF PIGS INVASION

. . . .

CUBAN MISSILE CRISIS

. . . .

BEATNIKS

PART
III

A CIA-sponsored invasion of Cuba in 1961 by 1,300 Cuban exiles attempting to overthrow the Castro regime. Cuban forces overwhelmed the invaders and easily stopped the plot. The incident sparked international outrage and embarrassed President Kennedy only weeks into his presidency.

. . . .

Standoff in October 1962 when the United States discovered that the Soviet Union was building nuclear missile launch sites in Cuba. President Kennedy ordered their removal and implemented a naval blockade of Cuba. Soviet leader Nikita Khrushchev eventually acquiesced. The incident is likely the closest that the United States came to war with the Soviet Union.

. . . .

A term used to describe bohemian writers and artists of the late 1940s and 1950s, such as Jack Kerouac (author of *On the Road*) and poet Allen Ginsberg.

CIVIL RIGHTS ACT OF 1964

. . . .

BETTY FRIEDAN

. . . .

CÉSAR CHÁVEZ

Outlawed racial and gender-based discrimination, which gave the government power to enforce racial integration in schools and fight discrimination at the workplace and public facilities.

• •

Feminist writer whose 1963 book, *The Feminine Mystique*, described the unhappiness of many women with society's traditional roles. Friedan noted that while women were as capable as men to achieve professional success, American society discouraged them from pursuing goals outside of marriage and motherhood.

• •

Civil rights and labor leader who in 1962 cofounded the National Farm Workers Association, an agricultural workers' union, and used nonviolent tactics on behalf of exploited Mexican-American farm workers.

NATIONAL ORGANIZATION OF WOMEN

. . . .

LYNDON BAINES JOHNSON

. . . .

THE GREAT SOCIETY

PART III

Founded by Betty Friedan in 1966, the group advocated for women's civil rights and a larger role for women in a male-dominated society.

• •

Thirty-sixth president (1963–1969); remembered for encouraging U.S. involvement in Vietnam, his Great Society domestic platform expanded civil rights and upheld Medicare, Medicaid, and environmental protection.

• •

Name for the social reforms of President Johnson's administration, which focused on eliminating racial discrimination and poverty. Many Great Society programs, such as Medicare and Medicaid, still exist.

MEDICARE

. . . .

EQUAL EMPLOYMENT
OPPORTUNITY COMMISSION

. . . .

AFFIRMATIVE ACTION

PART
III

A national health insurance program born as part of President Johnson's Great Society legislation that guarantees medical care for Americans over the age of 65.

. . . .

Established by LBJ, this commission enforces laws against workplace discrimination based on gender, ethnicity, race, or religion.

. . . .

Policies originating in the Johnson administration to create an equal opportunity for blacks and women. The government encouraged employers and colleges to hire or accept minorities and women. Some Americans felt these policies were a form of reverse discrimination.

MALCOLM X

. . . .

DOMINO THEORY

PART
III

. . . .

VIETNAM WAR

African-American civil rights activist considered more militant than colleagues like Dr. Martin Luther King, Jr., he headed the controversial Nation of Islam and later, the Organization of Afro-American Unity. Three members of the group assassinated Malcolm X in 1965.

· ·

The Cold War theory that if one country succumbs to a communist revolution, neighboring countries will fall into communism like dominoes. This theory was one rationale for the war in Vietnam.

· ·

Cold War-era conflict between North Vietnam, backed by communist allies, and South Vietnam, supported by the United States as part of the containment strategy. The United States never formally declared war against North Vietnam, though American troops fought in the region for nearly a decade until 1973.

GULF OF TONKIN RESOLUTION

. . . .

HO CHI MINH

. . . .

VIETCONG

Passed by Congress in 1964, the resolution supported President Johnson in taking military action to prevent the further spread of communism in South Vietnam. The resolution gave Johnson the ability to use military force in Vietnam without a formal declaration of war.

· ·

President of North Vietnam, 1954–1969, he organized and supported the Vietcong against South Vietnam and commanded North Vietnamese troops in the Vietnam war.

· ·

The Communist-led political organization and militia who fought against both the United States and the South Vietnamese government during the Vietnam war. Known for guerilla fighting techniques.

HO CHI MINH TRAIL

. . . .

ANTIWAR MOVEMENT

. . . .

STUDENTS FOR A DEMOCRATIC
SOCIETY (SDS)

PART
III

Connected the North Vietnamese supply lines with Vietcong fighters in South Vietnam.

• •

In response to what many saw as an unnecessary war in Vietnam, Americans protested the conflict (and the compulsory draft) through walkouts, marches, protests, sit-ins, teach-ins, and participation in antiwar organizations.

• •

Radical youth activist group calling for an end to militarism, materialism, and racial segregation, they became increasingly militant and chapters of the group occupied college campus buildings.

TET OFFENSIVE

. . . .

MY LAI MASSACRE

. . . .

ROBERT KENNEDY

In January 1968, on Tet (the Vietnamese New Year), Vietcong troops launched a surprise attack on American troops and bases and fought from small villages to the city of Saigon. The attack soured American public opinion of the war.

. . . .

The massacre of several hundred Vietnamese civilians (mostly women, children, and the elderly) by U.S. troops in 1968. Discovery of the massacre inflamed antiwar sentiment in the United States.

. . . .

President Kennedy's younger brother and U.S. Attorney General was assassinated in 1968 while campaigning for the Democratic presidential nomination.

BLACK PANTHERS

. . . .

DETROIT RACE RIOTS

PART III

. . . .

STONEWALL RIOTS

Black militant group led by Bobby Seale and Huey Newton who believed that American capitalist society was inherently racist. They upheld black self-sufficiency and socialist revolution.

. . . .

The most severe of nationwide race riots during the late 1960s, this five-day skirmish in 1967 between black citizens and Detroit police began when a hostile crowd confronted officers arresting black patrons at an after-hours bar. The riots caused the deaths of 43 people, over 7,000 arrests, and the destruction of 2,000 buildings. Similar riots afflicted other American cities.

. . . .

Violent demonstrations in response to police raiding a New York City club frequented by gay men. The event marked the beginning of the gay rights movement in the United States.

HIPPIES

. . . .

COUNTERCULTURE

. . . .

WOODSTOCK

Youth subculture of the 1960s that embraced psychedelic music, recreational drug use, and the sexual revolution. The hippies had a broad cultural influence and close political ties to the antiwar movement.

. . . .

Term used to describe a set of attitudes, beliefs, and way of life that run against mainstream society. In America, the term most often refers to the youth culture of the 1960s that introduced new artistic styles and permissive attitudes about sexuality and drug use.

. . . .

The defining moment in the musical counter-culture, a three-day festival in 1969 held in upstate New York featuring musicians like Janis Joplin and Jimi Hendrix.

KENT STATE MASSACRE

. . . .

TWENTY-SIXTH AMENDMENT

. . . .

SILENT MAJORITY

PART III

The 1970 killing by the National Guard of four unarmed students protesting the United States invasion of Cambodia. The incident sparked national outrage and strengthened the anti-war movement.

. . . .

Ratified in 1971, this amendment officially lowered the voting age from 21 to 18. The amendment was a direct response to student involvement in the antiwar movement.

. . . .

In 1969, Nixon referred to the many voters who would sweep him into the presidency as a "silent majority," as they did not participate in the counterculture or participate in protests.

RICHARD NIXON

. . . .

VIETNAMIZATION

PART
III

. . . .

DETENTE

Thirty-seventh president (1969–1974); ended the unsuccessful war in Vietnam, negotiated toward detente with the USSR, opened political relations with China; best remembered for involvement in Watergate scandal, which forced him to be the first president to resign.

• •

Nixon's policy to reduce the role of American troops in Vietnam by leaving increasing combat responsibilities to the South Vietnamese. Following the Tet Offensive, the gradual withdrawal of American troops lasted over five years.

• •

This term refers to the relaxing of tensions during the Cold War beginning in 1971. The policies associated with detente included a pause in the arms race and treaties to reduce nuclear arsenals. The phase ended with Ronald Reagan's election.

SALT

· ·

SPACE RACE

· ·

APOLLO 11

Strategic Arms Limitation Talks, bilateral meet-
ings between the United States and the Soviet
Union to reduce nuclear arms, which reflects
Nixon's detente policy. The first talks in 1973
led to the Anti-Ballistic Missile Treaty, but the
United States eventually withdrew from the
second round of talks.

. . . .

The competition during the 1950s and 1960s
between the United States and the USSR to
become the leader of space exploration. The
Soviets launched the first satellite, Sputnik,
and put the first man in space. American John
Glenn was the first man to orbit Earth, and the
American Apollo 11 mission brought the first
men to the moon in 1969.

. . . .

This NASA mission in 1969 brought astronauts
Neil Armstrong and Buzz Aldrin to the moon
while a captivated world watched live on
television.

SPIRO AGNEW

. . . .

WATERGATE

. . . .

CLEAN AIR ACT

Nixon's first vice president, Agnew was forced to resign in 1973 when he was charged with accepting bribes. Nixon replaced him with Gerald Ford.

. . . .

A series of political scandals that began when five burglars were caught attempting to wiretap the offices of the Democratic National Committee. It was later discovered that President Nixon attempted to hide his involvement in the plot, which led to his resignation on August 9, 1974.

. . . .

A federal law passed in 1963 and since amended several times that empowers the federal government to regulate industrial air pollution.

ROE v. WADE

. . . .

GERALD FORD

. . . .

HELSINKI ACCORDS

PART
III

The 1973 Supreme Court ruling that made it legal for a woman to have an abortion, which became a defining political divide between liberals and conservatives for decades to come.

• •

Thirty-eighth president (1974–1977); pardoned Nixon for his involvement in Watergate; presided over a stagnant economy spurred by an oil crisis in the Middle East and high inflation; signed the Helsinki Accords, which furthered the American policy of detente.

• •

Agreement between major world powers in 1975 to respect sovereignty and seek peaceful resolution of disputes.

1973 OIL CRISIS

. . . .

INFLATION

. . . .

STAGFLATION

PART
III

When oil-exporting Middle Eastern nations banded together to cut oil production in response to American support of Israel during the Yom Kippur War, the price of oil shot up, exacerbating economic turmoil in the United States and many industrialized countries.

· ·

An increase in the amount of money in circulation, resulting in the currency having a lower value. Rising costs on goods are often associated with inflation.

· ·

An economic event combining high inflation, high employment, and slow economic growth. This presents a challenge to policymakers, as traditional economic stimuli, such as lowering inflation, could raise unemployment during stagflation. The global economy entered a period of stagflation in the mid-1970s.

JIMMY CARTER

. . . .

THREE MILE ISLAND

. . . .

IRANIAN REVOLUTION

Thirty-ninth president (1977–1981); signed the landmark Camp David Accords for Middle East peace; presided over worldwide economic stagflation due in part to the energy crisis; failed to secure release of American hostages in Iran; created the departments of Energy and Education.

. . . .

Pennsylvania site of a partial nuclear meltdown at a power plant, the worst such accident in American history. The incident irreparably harmed the nuclear power industry in the United States.

. . . .

A conservative backlash against the Western-backed Shah of Iran led by the Ayatollah Khomeini. The 1979 revolution replaced the secular government with an Islamic theocracy opposed to American interests.

IRAN HOSTAGE CRISIS

. . . .

CAMP DAVID ACCORDS

. . . .

MORAL MAJORITY

PART
III

During the Iranian revolution in 1979, Iranians seized the U.S. embassy and held 52 Americans as hostages for over a year. A failed rescue attempt in 1980 resulted in the deaths of eight servicemen.

. . . .

Mediated by President Carter, this 1979 peace agreement between Israel and Egypt reduced tensions between the two most powerful militaries in the Middle East.

. . . .

Political organization of evangelical Christians founded in 1979 by Jerry Falwell to lobby for religious values.

RONALD REAGAN

. . . .

REAGAN REVOLUTION

. . . .

REAGANOMICS

PART III

Fortieth president (1981–1989); former movie star; his economic reforms known as "Reaganomics" reduced taxes to promote economic growth; repudiated detente and invested in arms buildup; remembered for sparking conservative ideological revolution and also the Iran-Contra crisis; also accused of ignoring the AIDS crisis and deteriorating inner cities.

• •

Refers to the rapid political realignment of the United States toward conservatism and free-market economics as a result of Reagan's presidency.

• •

President Reagan's economic reforms aimed to reduce government spending, lower income tax and capital gains taxes, control the money supply to reduce inflation, and lessen government regulation of the economy.

SUPPLY-SIDE ECONOMICS

. . . .

RUST BELT

. . . .

SERVICE ECONOMY

PART
III

Reagan's economics theory that allowing large companies to make profits will lead them to invest and stimulate the economy.

. . . .

A term for the former metals and manufacturing hub in the Midwest. Local economies in these regions depended on manufacturing and raw materials processing, yet these industries moved to other states or even foreign countries where labor is cheaper. Declining employment in the Rust Belt captures the transformation of the United States economy.

. . . .

The service sector replaced manufacturing and agriculture as the crucial segment of the American economy during the late twentieth century. Instead of harvesting or building, more American workers were involved in the production of services rather than physical goods. Such services might be the transport, distribution, and sale of products (the retail industry), or providing information or knowledge (advertising, marketing, communications).

GERALDINE FERRARO

. . . .

SANDRA DAY O'CONNOR

. . . .

WAR ON DRUGS

PART
III

Congresswoman who became the first woman on a major-party presidential ticket when Democrat Walter Mondale chose her as his vice presidential candidate in 1984. Mondale and Ferraro lost when Reagan was reelected.

• •

Nominated by President Reagan in 1981, O'Connor was the first female Supreme Court Justice.

• •

The American effort to curb drug imports and abuse. Originating in the Nixon administration, this ongoing effort involves military and monetary assistance to foreign governments and stringent antidrug laws in the United States. These controversial laws have dramatically increased the number of Americans in prison or jail, with inner-city minority populations heavily affected.

AIDS CRISIS

. . . .

YUPPIES

. . . .

PERSONAL COMPUTER

PART III

The symptoms of the virus that would later become known as HIV/AIDS were first seen in a dozen people in New York and San Francisco in 1981. Today, the disease has killed an estimated 25 million people.

• •

From an abbreviation for young urban professionals, the term refers to the generation of young adults in the 1980s considered to be materialistic, pursuing wealth and social status through conspicuous consumption.

• •

Affordable and user-friendly PCs developed by companies like IBM and Apple and running software by Microsoft revolutionized information storage and communication in almost every profession.

CHALLENGER DISASTER

. . . .

IRAN-CONTRA AFFAIR

. . . .

MIKHAIL GORBACHEV

PART III

The space shuttle Challenger exploded 73 seconds after takeoff in 1986, killing all seven American astronauts. The disaster forced the suspension of the space shuttle program for nearly three years and immeasurably damaged American investment in space exploration.

• •

Political scandal in 1986 when the Reagan administration ignored a Congressional ruling by selling weapons to Iran in order to gain funds for anti-Communist forces in Nicaragua.

• •

Soviet leader who pursued more open domestic and foreign policies that ended the Cold War and led to the dissolution of the Soviet Union.

GEORGE H.W. BUSH

. . . .

PERSIAN GULF WAR

. . . .

L.A. RIOTS

PART III

Forty-first president (1989–1993); oversaw the end of the Cold War; led the nation into the Persian Gulf War to repel the Iraqi invasion of Kuwait; father of President George W. Bush.

• •

A war between a U.S.-led coalition and Iraq following Iraq's invasion of Kuwait, an oil-rich kingdom in the Persian Gulf. American victory was swift and decisive, though Iraqi dictator Saddam Hussein was allowed to remain in power until another U.S.-led war in 2003.

• •

Six days of violent looting and violence in Los Angeles during the spring of 1992 after a jury acquitted white police officers in the beating of Rodney King, an African-American man. The riots claimed over 50 lives, caused $2 billion in property damage, and served as a symbol of a persisting racial divide.

BILL CLINTON

. . . .

ELECTION OF 2000

. . . .

SEPTEMBER 11TH ATTACKS

PART
III

Forty-second president (1993–2001), the first of the baby boomer generation; signed landmark free-trade agreement NAFTA, presided over a period of economic prosperity with low interest rates, unemployment, and inflation. Clinton became the second president to be impeached after a 1998 perjury scandal, though he was acquitted by the Senate and remained in office.

. . . .

Contentious election between Democrat Al Gore and Republican George W. Bush. Gore won the popular vote, but the election hinged on Florida's electoral votes. After several court cases related to recounting the Florida vote, the Supreme Court stopped the recounts, awarding the state to Bush.

. . . .

Terrorist attacks by Islamic fundamentalist group Al-Qaeda resulting in the destruction of New York's World Trade Center and damage to the Pentagon in Washington by crashing hijacked airplanes. Passengers retaliated on another plane—intended for a target in Washington, D.C.—that crashed in Pennsylvania. Approximately 3,000 people died in the attacks, which sparked the War on Terror.